DYNAMIC LEA

A DISRUPTIVE WORLD

FRANS CAMPHER

Printed in the United Kingdom

First Printing: August 2025

Published by: Freedom Education Inc.

ISBN: 978-1-0683658-0-5 (Paperback)
ISBN: 978-1-0683658-1-2 (Electronic Book)
ISBN: 978-1-0683658-2-9 (Audio)

This book may be purchased for educational, business or sales promotional use. Special discounts are available on quantity purchases. For more information, please email.

Email: frans@ildynamics.com

DISCLAIMER

While the author and publisher have strived to be as accurate and complete as possible in the creation of this book, readers are cautioned to rely on their own judgment about their individual circumstances to act accordingly.

The author and publisher are providing this information on an educational basis and will not be liable for damages arising out of, or in connection with, the use of the content in this book. This is a comprehensive limitation of liability that applies to all damages of any kind, including (without limitation) compensatory; direct, indirect or direct, indirect or consequential damages; loss of data, income or profit; loss of or damage to property and claims of third parties.

While all attempts have been made to verify information provided in this publication, the author and publisher assumes no responsibility for errors, omissions, or contrary interpretation of the subject matter herein. Any perceived slights of specific persons, peoples, or organizations are unintentional. This book details the author's own personal experiences and opinions.

DEDICATION

To my beloved wife and co-founder, Debbie Campher:

For over 20 years, you were the heart of Integral Leadership Dynamics. Your wisdom, vision, and unwavering dedication to our clients created a legacy of lasting partnerships and meaningful impact. You continue to inspire me, and I am forever guided by the light you brought to everything you touched.

In loving memory of our co-founder ***Debbie Campher***
Soulmate, Sister, Mum, Aunt, Business Partner and our "Yoda".
09/07/1963 to 25/06/2023

TABLE OF CONTENTS

CHAPTER 3:
Leading With Integrity: Discovering Your Purpose And Core Values 31

FOREWORD

What makes Frans Campher such a compelling teacher is that he lives what he teaches. Dynamic Leadership is not just a book filled with insights - it is a direct expression of how Frans shows up in the world. His writing, his teaching, and his presence are fully aligned: grounded in integrity, rich with real-world wisdom, and deeply human.

Whether in a coaching session, on a stage, or through the pages of this book, Frans invites others into leadership that is both authentic and courageous. He doesn't just talk about shedding the masks or leading with purpose - he models it. This rare consistency is what builds deep trust and lasting impact with everyone he works with.

Reading Dynamic Leadership is like spending time with Frans himself: honest, generous, practical, and quietly transformative.

Dr Mark Jenner
Visting Fellow
Imperial College London

INTRODUCTION:

THE FIRST STEP: LEADING WITH AUTHENTICITY IN A DISRUPTIVE WORLD

Knowing yourself is the beginning of all wisdom.
–Aristotle

Today, leadership requires more than competence or strategy. It demands authenticity. In a world defined by disruption and rapid change, the most effective leaders are those who show up as their true selves. But how do you do this when expectations, self-doubt, and external pressures weigh you down? This book is your guide to reclaiming the power of being yourself and leading with integrity.

Years ago I found myself at a crossroads. I was running a European insurance broking company and tensions with the organization had been simmering for some time. Then, one of my team members was dishonest with a client. I took the fall as the incident happened on my watch. This was a breaking point for me.

Soon after, I was offered a job with a competitor. On paper, it was everything I thought I wanted. It was a chance to move on and rebuild elsewhere. But for some reason I let the contract sit on my desk in my home office for three days. Something in me hesitated. When my late wife Deb noticed the offer letter sitting on my desk, we had a conversation I'll never forget.

I told Deb I wasn't sure I wanted to go back to doing what I'd always done. Always insightful, she asked, "What do you love to do every day?" Without hesitation, I knew the answer. "I love to support people in their growth and development."

"Well why don't we do that all the time?" she asked. That moment of clarity was the spark we needed. Deb and I decided to take a leap of faith, sell our house, and start over. Together, we embarked on a journey of reinvention.

Have you ever felt stuck or questioned whether you're too focused on merely meeting the expectations of others? These moments of doubt can feel overwhelming. Yet they often hold the seeds of transformation. For me, such a moment marked the beginning of a journey that reshaped my life.

This book will show you how to identify what's holding you back, build unshakable trust in yourself, and lead with integrity in every aspect of your life. Through practical tools, personal stories, and actionable strategies, you'll discover how authenticity can transform your leadership and inspire those around you to thrive.

Whether you're navigating workplace disruption, striving to build trust within your team, or seeking to align your actions with your values, this journey starts with one simple realization: *you are enough*. When you lead with authenticity, you unlock not only your own potential but also the collective strength of those around you.

Let's take the first step together.

CHAPTER 1:

UNMASKING LEADERSHIP: THE JOURNEY TO TRUE INFLUENCE

Flexibility comes from having multiple choices; wisdom comes from having multiple perspectives. –Robert Dilts

Not long after my conversation with Deb, I enrolled in a nine-month practitioner program in Neuro-Linguistic Programming (NLP), a methodology that explores the connection between neurological processes, language, and behavioral patterns. It focuses on how individuals can reframe their thoughts and communication to achieve personal and professional goals, often promoting profound transformation.

The first module was eye-opening. I immediately sensed I was on the brink of significant personal growth. However, something felt incomplete. I couldn't imagine continuing the program without Deb by my side. So, I withdrew, intending to return when we could be on this journey together. Before long, Deb joined me, and from that moment, we committed to growing in tandem. Together, we completed the NLP practitioner program, the master practitioner training, and a coaching certification. Sharing every step of our personal development journey laid the foundation for what would eventually become our business.

Deb and I brought complementary strengths of clarity, structure, creativity, and the ability to make a meaningful impact. Our synergy didn't go unnoticed. Ian McDermott of International Teaching Seminars (ITS), who led much of our training, began mentoring us. In exchange, we volunteered our time and skills for his programs, soaking up everything we could about his business.

One day, during a seminar, someone in the audience approached us with an unexpected request: to develop a coaching program for his organization. We had no blueprint, no plan, but we said yes. That sparked a business that has since trained thousands of people across the globe. Did we know it would turn out this way? Not entirely. But we believed in the possibility, and that belief was enough to make it happen.

Today, our mission is clear: to empower leaders to show up authentically, build trust, and create lasting impact. In an age of constant change and complexity, leaders are often pulled in multiple directions, whether it's shifting workplace cultures, external expectations, or their own internal doubts. This book is here to help you cut through the noise, embrace your unique strengths, and lead with integrity in a world that desperately needs it.

The First Step: Trusting Yourself

This journey of transformation didn't happen overnight. It began with a simple yet profound realization: *I'm OK.* This foundational stage is when you learn to trust yourself, to feel safe in your own skin, and to embrace who you truly are.

Being yourself feels profoundly empowering. This spills over into your professional life, your personal relationships, and even into the way you interact with family and friends. Without the need to wear masks, you begin to show up consistently as your true self, which in turn builds trust and creates safety for those around you.

With this level of self-trust, a new identity starts to emerge, one that allows you to add value in ways you hadn't imagined. This value doesn't come from external validation. It doesn't come from your leadership team, your spouse, or even the CEO. It comes from within. It becomes the driving force for deeper, more meaningful relationships.

As you begin to trust yourself more, your relationships evolve. You stop trying to do everything on your own and become an enabler for others. You create space for those around you to feel "OK" too. This shift from needing to prove your worth to empowering others to thrive unlocks the collective potential of your teams and organization. In this way, authentic leadership is not about control or perfection; it's about showing up as your whole self and creating the conditions for others to do the same.

Overcoming Thought Viruses: Reclaiming Your Authentic Self

Embracing authenticity isn't without its challenges. Along the way, I encountered mental roadblocks, often described by Robert Dilts, a renowned pioneer in NLP, as "thought viruses."[1] Dilts developed this concept to explain the insidious patterns of doubt and fear that undermine confidence and cloud judgment. Recognizing and addressing these thought viruses is essential to freeing yourself from their grip.

One of the most common thought viruses is the feeling of being "not good enough." It manifests as a nagging doubt: *"Am I qualified to be here? What if someone finds out I'm not?"* This sense of imposter syndrome often affects leaders in pivotal positions, regardless of their accomplishments. These thoughts are not inherently yours. They are intruders, beliefs absorbed from external pressures or past experiences.

Imagine an executive who has climbed the ranks but still wonders, *"Do I belong here?"* This doubt is pervasive

[1] Dilts, Robert. "Thought Viruses, Mental Maps and Health." *Anchor Point*, March-April 1996.

and self-reinforcing, leading to a fear of being exposed as inadequate. It's a thought virus, not a truth. The first step to overcoming it is awareness, that is, recognizing that these thoughts are external and not an accurate reflection of your capabilities.

Another common scenario is the subtle sexism that women in leadership roles often face. Consider a situation where a woman earns a promotion. Male colleagues might dismiss her success, attributing it to diversity quotas rather than merit. Women, in turn, may question their worth, echoing the unfounded doubts of others. This external bias can plant an internal thought virus: *"Did I really deserve this?"*

The key to overcoming these thought viruses is reframing the narrative. Instead of asking, *"Am I good enough?"* assert, *"I earned this. I belong here."* By recognizing the virus for the distortion it is you can replace it with a mindset rooted in confidence and authenticity.

Letting Go of the Need to Please

Another destructive thought virus centers on the need for approval: *"Do people like me?"* Leaders often fall into the trap of making decisions based on popularity rather than what is right for their teams or organizations. This habit of people-pleasing can lead to bending your values and priorities to align with others' expectations, compromising your authenticity.

For instance, a leader focused on being liked may avoid making tough decisions, opting instead for easier, expedient choices. While this may momentarily satisfy those around them, it undermines long-term trust and respect. Decisions made to gain approval often prioritize personal comfort over organizational goals, weakening the leader's credibility.

To counteract this thought virus, adjust your focus from popularity to respect. Ask yourself, *"Am I acting in a way that aligns with my values and earns the respect of my team?"*

Releasing the need to please also requires a change in perspective. Instead of asking, *"Do they like me?"* consider, *"Am I creating value and fostering trust?"* This realignment not only strengthens your leadership but also empowers your team to operate authentically, free from the weight of constant validation-seeking.

The Path to Freedom: Owning Your Authenticity

Letting go of thought viruses begins with a powerful realization: *Being myself is enough.* When you accept that you are worthy as you are, you no longer need to wear masks or bend yourself to fit others' expectations. This creates consistency, allowing you to show up as the same person in every context, whether in the boardroom, with your team, or at home.

The day you decide to stop being someone else and start embracing your true self is the day you unlock your potential as a leader. It's not just liberating; it's transformative. You become someone who leads from a place of inner confidence and trust, inspiring others to do the same.

The Exhaustion of Wearing Masks

As I progressed in my career, I achieved what many would consider a dream role. I was headhunted from the second-largest insurance broking organization in South Africa to the largest in the UK, where I was placed on the board. It was an exciting opportunity, but was not without its challenges.

As an outsider in the UK market, my appointment raised eyebrows. Board members questioned, *"Who is this guy? Why did he get this job?"* It wasn't long before I discovered that some of my colleagues had a bet going, wagering that I wouldn't last a year in the London market. While outwardly I shrugged it off, internally I found myself bending and reshaping my identity to appease the skepticism around me.

In my efforts to navigate these dynamics, I became a chameleon, constantly adapting to the expectations of those around me. With the board, I was Frans #1, formal and reserved. With my operational team, I was Frans #2, approachable and relatable. With the chairman, I became Frans #3, overly accommodating to avoid conflict. And at home, with my wife and family, I tried to leave it all behind, becoming yet another version of myself.

Each mask felt necessary at the time, but together, they became suffocating. I was always watching my words, curating my behavior, and striving to fit the context rather than showing up as my authentic self. It was exhausting. The constant shifting of identities began to wear me down, and I realized that this way of living was unsustainable.

The Cost of Shrinking Yourself

One moment stands out vividly in my memory. During a board meeting, I found myself being overly careful, editing my words, suppressing my opinions, and second-guessing my every move. Leadership expert Nancy Kline once said, *"Be careful about being yourself."* While her advice encourages thoughtfulness, I was taking it to an extreme. My carefulness turned into self-censorship, and my unique talents and ideas were buried beneath layers of appeasement.

In trying to fit in, I was shrinking myself. I wasn't just accommodating others; I was sacrificing my authenticity and, with it, my power as a leader. I could feel it happening, my voice growing quieter, my confidence waning. It wasn't just exhausting; it was counterproductive.

Recognizing the Masks Around Us

The truth is, we can all spot when someone is "playing a part." As human beings, we're wired to sense when someone is trying to project an image rather than being themselves. People tell stories that emphasize their strengths and gloss over their flaws, hoping to be seen, validated, and appreciated. While these behaviors may help them fit in momentarily, they often fail to build genuine trust or respect.

I saw this clearly in myself and realized I had to make a change. The toll of wearing multiple masks was too great. I needed to rediscover the Frans who didn't have to bend or reshape to fit every room. I needed to let go of the fear of judgment. I needed to believe that who I was, as I was, was enough.

This realization became a pivotal moment in my leadership journey. It taught me that from the boardroom to the dinner table, embracing consistency and integrity allows your true talents to shine through, creating deeper connections with those around you.

Date with Destiny: Embracing Authenticity

This change had been brewing for some time. At least a year before I left my career in insurance, Deb and I attended Tony Robbins' *Date with Destiny*. During one of the exercises, we were asked to define our purpose, identity, and who we wanted to be. As I reflected, a startling realization struck me: I was wasting enormous amounts of energy pretending to be different people in different contexts. I left that event with a new resolve. I decided that being me, unapologetically and consistently, was enough.

This decision was transformative. I no longer felt the need to bend myself out of shape to meet the false narratives that often thrive in toxic cultures. The relief was immediate and profound. Returning from the event, I decided to embrace authenticity in every aspect of my life. At work, this changed everything. I began to show up consistently, as the same person, regardless of the room or the audience.

This newfound clarity gave me the confidence to approach my boss with a bold proposal. I asked to take on a larger division within the organization. His initial response was measured: "Focus on running your division for now, and we'll revisit this in six months." I took that advice to heart, pouring my energy into leading my team authentically and effectively.

Six months later, my boss approached me and said, "Why don't you run all the divisions?" I said yes without hesitation. The promotion felt natural, not because I was trying to impress anyone, but because I had finally allowed myself to lead as my true self. My consistency built trust, and that translated into influence and success.

The results were undeniable. I became more effective, more influential, and was promoted more quickly than ever before. The lesson was clear: the world craves leaders who have the courage to show up authentically. Before attending *Date with Destiny*, I understood many of these ideas conceptually. But it wasn't until I experienced them firsthand that I learned how to make them real.

Rising Above the Past: Revealing Your True Self

This journey isn't about labeling thought viruses or using masks to appease others. It's about chiseling away at the past to uncover the authentic self that has always been there. True freedom comes from rising above these barriers, letting go of false identities, and embracing the purpose that lies beneath.

Living authentically is not easy, but it's worth it. It's about having the courage to be who you are. As you move through this book, you'll discover how to shed the thought viruses, masks, and self-doubts that hold you back, and replace them with a mindset rooted in trust and purpose. When you lead from this place, you not only transform yourself but also inspire those around you to do the same. Together, we can create a new generation of leaders who are bold, authentic, and ready to make a lasting impact. That's the kind of leadership the world truly needs.

KEY INSIGHTS:

- Leading authentically starts with removing the "masks" we wear to fit others' expectations, allowing us to show up consistently and build deeper trust.
- Recognizing and reframing thought viruses such as self-doubt, imposter syndrome, and the need for approval are critical steps toward reclaiming your true leadership potential.
- When leaders embrace who they truly are, they inspire trust, build stronger relationships, and activate the collective potential of their teams.

CHAPTER 2:

SHIFTING THE PARADIGM: FROM CHANGE MANAGEMENT TO LEADING CHANGE

The measure of intelligence is the ability to change.
–Albert Einstein

I have to admit, I can't stand the term *change management*. For one, it assumes that change comes from external forces. This approach often fails to deliver consistent or lasting results. Trying to convince someone to adopt a change that isn't their own idea is rarely effective. This is why so many change management programs fail: the people tasked with executing the change often lack the same level of commitment as those driving it forward.

Change management typically relies on forcing or convincing people to accept change rather than inspiring genuine buy-in. A striking example of its pitfalls comes from the National Health Service (NHS) in the United

Kingdom. In the early 2000s, the NHS invested a staggering 17.5 billion pounds in an attempt to centralize patient data. The problem wasn't the vision; it was the execution. The consultants drove the change from the top down, excluding the people closest to the work. Within seven years, the initiative collapsed. In short, it was a complete failure.

Change leadership requires a different approach, one grounded in collaboration and trust. Leaders who embrace this mindset inspire others to follow, not because they're told to, but because the team sees value in the change. It's not about managing tasks or imposing directives; it's about engaging people in a shared vision and empowering them to contribute meaningfully.

Why did it fail? For one, rather than engaging with those directly involved, the consultants approached the program with a top-down, instructional mindset. They told people what to do and how to do it. This created external pressure but failed to build the internal commitment necessary for success. The consultants never consulted the people on the ground, those collecting and managing the data, to understand their needs or gather insights on how the process could be improved. By excluding these key stakeholders, they undermined the very people whose buy-in was crucial, leading to resistance and ineffectiveness.

Too often, those in leadership positions make sweeping decisions without consulting the people closest to the work. They may justify this with urgency, claiming, "We need to be agile and make this happen quickly." Yet skipping collaboration almost guarantees push-back. Without engaging those most directly affected by the change and involving them in the process, there's no sense of ownership. And without ownership, true change is nearly impossible.

Leading Change from Within

Change must be led from within. That means engaging with stakeholders, actively seeking their input, and involving the people around you in the process. By doing so, you create a foundation of collaboration and commitment that drives meaningful and lasting transformation.

Leading change means inspiring others to follow not because they feel coerced or obligated, but because they have willingly agreed and are committed to your vision. It's about fostering an internal commitment where people actively choose to participate because they see value in the change and how it benefits them. When individuals feel ownership in the process, their engagement is genuine. Their efforts are wholehearted. Lasting change comes from individuals who are motivated to step up and be part of the transformation, not from those simply following orders.

The ability to lead change from within is a skill that can be learned, and fortunately it's not as difficult as it might seem. By involving your team and showing them how these changes will benefit and serve them, you create a deeper sense of ownership and commitment. When people see their input valued and understand the personal and collective advantages of the change, their engagement strengthens. This collaborative approach both accelerates the implementation process and ensures the change is more effective and sustainable.

True commitment to change must come from individuals, not simply from top-down directives. As an executive or CEO, you might argue, "It's our decision that change must take place." While that may be true, implementing change smoothly without the commitment of your team is nearly impossible. If you want outstanding results, you must involve your team in the decision-making process. Ask for their input, listen to their ideas, and show them how they can support and benefit from achieving the goal. This approach accelerates the delivery of change and reduces resistance, ultimately saving time and resources.

Some leaders dismiss this collaborative approach, believing there isn't time for "soft, cuddly conversations." Yet, forcing change without buy-in leads to superficial agreement rather than genuine commitment. When individuals feel the change is imposed upon them, it weakens their engagement, and the results fall short. Meaningful progress requires people to see themselves as part of the change, not as passive recipients of decisions made elsewhere.

How to Co-Create the Solution

Effective change begins with constructive dialogue. To lead a successful transformation, you must engage your team by discussing why the change is necessary, the benefits it will bring, and how it can be implemented effectively. Start by saying, "We need your support and ideas to help achieve what we're working toward." As a leader, explain why the change is so important and share your vision of its impact. Then, invite their input with questions like, "What are your ideas for how we can make this work in the best possible way?" This collaborative approach builds trust, ownership, and commitment.

A case in point is a client of mine who wanted to implement a new self-service model for Human Resources. The goal was to move HR professionals away from handling transactional tasks, like pay or contract issues, to focusing on strategic, consultative work. They asked me to guide the transition for 80 HR leaders worldwide. I proposed two key steps: first, one-on-one conversations with the 10 most senior leaders to understand their perspectives; second, creating regional focus groups to discuss the proposed changes, their potential impacts, and ideas for successful implementation.

The results were striking. During the focus groups, we gathered extensive feedback, identified concerns, and incorporated innovative solutions suggested by participants. These collaborative sessions strengthened buy-in and generated actionable ideas. Three months later, the change was launched, and within three days, the system was running smoothly, with no major disruptions.

In contrast, another division of the same organization focused solely on process and structure, neglecting the human element of co-creation, ownership, and accountability. By overlooking the importance of engaging their teams, their implementation took three additional months and faced far more challenges. The key difference was simple: they managed the change, while we led it from within.

At the conclusion of the project, three leaders independently shared similar sentiments: "I've been through large change programs before, but this is the first time anyone asked for my opinion on how we could make it work." Their feedback underscores the importance of involving your team from the start.

To co-create meaningful change, consider asking these questions:

- Why is the change necessary?
- How will this benefit everyone involved?
- What are your ideas for implementing this change?

- How can we involve you in the process?
- How can you provide a meaningful contribution?

By centering your efforts around these questions, you ensure that change is not something done *to* people, but something achieved *with* them. This approach fosters internal commitment and accelerates the path to lasting success.

Start with Why

Oftentimes, I will do the following exercise with a class of 50-60 people in a room. I'll say to them, "I'd like you to stand up and follow me, please." Maybe one or two people will stand up, but the majority of them stay sitting, and are saying to themselves quietly, "No, no, I'm not going to follow you and stand up until I know why I'm following you." This is why we always start with "why." If you want others to follow your lead, tell them *why* you're making the change first. Even if the change is not good for me or if it's a bit of a problem for me, if I know the why and I can see the rationale behind it, I am more likely to comply.

How Will This Benefit Everyone Involved?

Effective change benefits everyone it touches, from employees to customers to external stakeholders. When employees see that changes are designed to improve their work experience, customers receive better service, and the company grows stronger overall. By taking care of customers, you foster greater job security for employees and, ultimately, better financial outcomes for the organization. It's crucial to communicate that changes aren't just about disruption for the sake of disruption. Instead, they're aimed at creating shared value across all levels of the organization. Highlighting these benefits clearly helps gain quicker and stronger buy-in from your team.

Take, for example, my client who implemented a new HR self-service model. This transformation allowed HR professionals to move from handling routine administrative tasks to becoming strategic business partners. With the mundane work off their plates, they had more capacity to consult effectively, which led to improved services for their patients. Better patient care enhanced the organization's reputation and contributed to its financial success. This change didn't just streamline processes; it empowered employees, satisfied customers, and drove better outcomes for the company.

Engaging Your Team in the Process

Your team's ideas can be the cornerstone of successful change. When you invite people to share their input on implementation, you tap into their creativity and expertise. More importantly, you foster a sense of ownership and commitment to the change. People are far more likely to contribute their best efforts when they feel their ideas are valued and their voices are heard.

Consider the example of Delta Air Lines during its financial crisis in 2005. Facing Chapter 11 bankruptcy, COO Jim Whitehurst had to make difficult decisions about cost-cutting measures. When he informed employees, including the engineers, that workforce reductions were necessary to keep the company afloat, the engineers asked, "What do you need to save?" Whitehurst explained they needed to cut 20% of the workforce. Rather than simply accepting the situation, the engineers proposed an alternative: transitioning to a three-day workweek to achieve the same savings while preserving jobs. Whitehurst embraced their idea, and it was successfully implemented.

This example highlights the power of collaboration. Whitehurst had a vision for navigating the crisis, but the actionable solutions came from the engineers themselves. By giving them the space to propose ideas, he gained innovative solutions and his team's commitment to making the plan work. When people feel seen and heard, their sense of ownership grows. They become invested in the success of the change, leading to faster and more effective implementation. Allowing your team to co-create solutions ensures that the vision becomes a shared goal rather than a directive imposed from the top.

The Role of Disruption

Disruption is an inherent part of the cycle of change. The key to navigating it lies in our mindset. When we accept that change and disruption are natural, constant, and inevitable aspects of life on this planet, we can approach them with greater ease. Embracing this perspective allows us to not only adapt to disruption but also to harness its potential for growth and transformation.

We are all constantly faced with these universal cycles of change. It happens in relationships. It happens at work and in business. It happens with technology. Nokia and BlackBerry dominated the phone market during the mid-to-late 2000s. You could make phone calls and send texts with those technologies. However, once Apple's smartphone was released in 2007, it completely disrupted those technologies. All of a sudden, we had a mini-computer in our hands. We were still making phone calls and sending texts. But we were also exchanging media and connecting to the Internet. The Nokias and BlackBerrys of our world were not able to adequately adapt to this change and perished as a result.

We are now in the fourth industrial revolution. Generative Artificial Intelligence (AI) and the adoption of this technology are accelerating at a fast pace. Jobs are being disrupted by the use of AI. We're in the middle of that disruption right now, and the biggest risk each individual faces is that they won't adapt to this change.

You have to understand that the purpose of disruption is to gently force us to evolve and grow personally and professionally. What we have to do in the face of disruption is ask ourselves: How do we add the value needed to the end result of AI? How do I make the best out of this? How do I benefit from this change? What is the opportunity? This shift in mindset will help you navigate disruption in a new way. Instead of being fearful or anxious, you'll be excited by what you can do to contribute to this major shift.

The biggest obstacle you'll ever face is not disruption itself. It's your inability to accept the change and look for the opportunity in it. The real challenge arises when you get too comfortable. Like the seasons, change is constant and never-ending. In the face of disruption, you need to ask yourself: What's the benefit of getting out of my comfort zone? What do I gain from it? Often it allows you to develop new capacities, build strengths, and discover ways to create value that didn't exist before.

A Catalyst for Growth

The truth is that disruption is here to support us. It's here to guide us and make our lives better. There is always a benefit. Today's smartphones have more computing power than the Apollo 13 spacecraft from 1970. If the Apollo missions had access to today's technology, spaceflight and communication would have been far simpler and more reliable. New technology serves humanity in profound ways. Never forget that.

The best thing you can do is embrace the universal truth that cycles of change will continue for centuries, long after you are gone. The planets will keep spinning, and the sun will keep rising. There is nothing you can do to change that. What you can do is choose to accept cycles of change, just as nature does. You never see trees bending over to pick up their fallen leaves.

Once you accept that disruption is a permanent part of life, you can begin to see these cycles of change as opportunities. You can choose to fight and resist the change, or you can embrace the opportunities it presents. The decision is yours. In every moment, you have the power to decide how you perceive your circumstances. Ask yourself: *Is this disruption an opportunity? What opportunities can I find in it? Will I resist this change or accept it?*

The choice is always yours. You can resist change, clinging to old patterns, or you can embrace it as an opportunity for growth and transformation. While authenticity forms the foundation of impactful leadership, it's only the beginning. The ability to navigate change and inspire others to join you demands more than just self-awareness. It requires practical tools and strategies that turn intention into action.

In the next chapter, we'll explore these tools and how to apply them to make the transition from simply managing change to truly leading it. Together, we'll dive into actionable approaches for fostering collaboration, building trust, and creating genuine commitment within your team. By doing so, you'll unlock the potential for transformation, both for yourself and those you lead.

KEY INSIGHTS:

- Engagement drives change. Involving stakeholders in the process fosters ownership, reduces resistance, and ensures lasting results.
- Leadership inspires, not imposes. Effective leaders focus on collaboration and commitment instead of top-down management.
- Disruption sparks growth. Embracing disruption allows leaders to adapt, innovate, and turn challenges into progress.

CHAPTER 3:

LEADING WITH INTEGRITY: DISCOVERING YOUR PURPOSE AND CORE VALUES

Authenticity is the daily practice of letting go of who we think we're supposed to be and embracing who we are.
–Brené Brown

Imagine a moment when you faced a critical decision that tested your core values. Were you willing to stand up for what you believed, even if it cost you? Every leader encounters these moments where purpose and integrity meet at a crossroads. The path you choose to take defines who you are as a leader. Authentic leadership isn't about perfection or pleasing everyone; it's about the courage to lead from your true self, no matter the stakes.

When I first came to London I inherited a small team of five. One team member stood out right away. He was a top performer but his approach didn't align with the teamwork-focused culture I wanted to build. From my first week on the job, it was clear he preferred to work independently, often prioritizing his own methods over the team's goals. While he brought strong skills to the table, his resistance to collaboration created friction within the group.

This guy was the top producer in the company. He was the best of the best. A few months into my new role, I spoke with him and said, "The game we are playing here is about being a team. This is how we play. It's not an individual game. It's a team game. You need to decide if you're willing to play as part of this team. If not, then we need to have a different discussion."

Three days after our conversation, he came to me and said, "I've decided to leave." I looked at him and replied, "I understand, and I respect your honesty." And with that, he left the company.

Later that day, the chairman called me, furious. "What the hell are you doing?" he demanded. "I heard you got rid of our best performer." I took a deep breath and said, "No, I asked him to play as part of a team, and he chose not to. He made the decision to leave because he didn't want to work that way."

The chairman wasn't convinced. "Do you know what you've done to us?" he asked, incredulous. "Yes," I replied calmly. "You put me in charge of this business. If, in six months, this doesn't work out, fire me. I'll move on. But I believe this is the right choice for the team."

About six months later, the chairman phoned me up again. This time, his tone was different. "I see what you mean," he admitted. "You were absolutely right. You made the right decision."

That choice proved itself: our team had come together in a powerful way, producing far beyond what a single high performer could achieve. By building a cohesive team, we operated more effectively and achieved remarkable results. Some board members had initially thought I was nuts. With time, however, they recognized the wisdom of the decision. They respected that I stood by my values, even under pressure.

This experience taught me something crucial: leadership isn't just about results; it's about standing for something. When you show your true values and honor who you are, you inspire others to do the same.

Standing for What Matters

You can't be yourself at the cost of everything else. You need to be in tune with yourself so that you know what is acceptable to you and what is not, and then you want to stand up for what you believe is right. Many years ago, when I was running an organization, I had a frank conversation with the board from day one about how bonuses would be structured and what it would take to achieve them. We set ambitious goals, knowing it would demand a lot from our team to meet them, but we all agreed to the terms. With the structure in place, we got to work, knowing that delivering on those promises would be no small feat.

Toward the end of the year, the Chairman approached me. "Look," he started, shifting uncomfortably, "we can't pay your people what we owe them because the rest of the organization didn't perform well."

I stared at him, shocked. "What? That's your fault, not mine. I have no control over what the rest of the company does. My team exceeded every expectation set for us."

"Thank God for your group, or we'd be in deep trouble," he replied.

I could feel irritation bubbling up. "And you're saying that to justify not paying them what they're owed?"

The Chairman nodded slightly, but it only made me more upset. "I'm not going to tell my team we can't pay their bonuses. They worked their butts off to deliver, and now you're trying to backtrack on what we agreed? I won't do it."

He sighed. "This decision comes from the board."

"Then I guess I'm in trouble because I won't stand by it," I told him. "I'm not just being difficult here. I'm standing up for what's right."

The Courage to Stand for Your Team

I had a purpose. I made a promise to my employees, and I was determined to keep it. For me, this was non-negotiable. You don't promise people a reward for meeting specific targets, then deny them that reward once they deliver.

I was fighting for my reputation and my integrity. I had personally negotiated the bonus structure with the board and our team, so I had skin in the game. More than that, though, I was standing up for my people. We set clear targets, and they met those targets. Breaking that promise would be unfair, and I wasn't willing to do it. So, I stood my ground and told the board, "I don't like it."

I wasn't going to compromise my principles by simply agreeing with the Chairman just because he was in a position of authority. If my values and purpose don't align with the organization's direction, I believe it's my responsibility to speak up. If you're reading this book, you probably do, too. In this case, I knew that if I didn't push back, nothing would change.

I went back and forth with the board, challenging them on why they couldn't honor the promised bonuses. Eventually, they saw the logic. We worked together to find a way to make the numbers work, juggling funds and negotiating a fair solution for everyone involved.

In the end, we were able to keep our promise, and my team received the bonuses they had earned.

When Conflict Reveals True Values

The lesson for me was that it's okay to be a rebel. Just don't be a rebel without a cause. Don't fight just for the sake of fighting; fight when something truly goes against your values or your larger purpose. Often, you won't fully understand what you stand for until those values are tested under pressure, as mine were in this situation. Just as diamonds form under intense pressure, who you truly are often emerges in moments of conflict.

Stand firm in what aligns with your true values, but remember there are many other perspectives and ways of seeing the world. My worldview may not match yours exactly, yet that doesn't mean I must conform if it goes against my own beliefs. For me, the choice was clear. I wasn't willing to compromise on what I knew was best for my team. I felt a responsibility to ensure they were recognized for the hard work they put in to earn those bonuses and wanted them to be rewarded fairly for their contributions.

As I learned through my experience with the board, staying true to your values often requires courage and resilience, especially when under pressure. And to consistently act in alignment with what matters most, you need a deep awareness of your core values and an honest look at where you might be compromising them.

Authenticity in Action

The following *Authenticity Audit* is a practical tool to help you identify areas in your life where you might be holding back from being your true self. By reflecting on your decisions and interactions, you can pinpoint situations where you may have felt compelled to act against your authentic nature. This exercise will guide you through steps to uncover the root causes, clarify your true intentions, and create a plan to bring more authenticity into your actions.

Authenticity Audit

Step	**Your Response**
Step 1: Reflect on Recent Decisions: *Identify a recent decision or interaction where you didn't feel fully authentic. What did you say or do? Did you feel like you were wearing a "hat" or playing a role?*	

Step 2: Identify the Root Cause: *Consider why you felt the need to act this way. Was it fear of judgment? Desire to fit in? Pressure to perform?*	
Step 3: Define Your Authentic Response *Write down what you would have said or done if you had been completely true to yourself.*	
Step 4: Create an Action Plan *Choose one small change to start practicing in similar situations.*	

Uncovering Hidden Commitments: Why Change Feels So Hard

Years ago, I was offered a role as chief executive at a time when my children were between the ages of 12 and 14. I was very close to my wife and family, and this new position would have meant spending three weeks each month on the road, essentially living on airplanes as I traveled to different cities. Taking on this role would mean missing out on my sons' lives. One was playing soccer, and the other was active in cricket and rugby. Faced with this competing commitment, I ultimately decided to turn down the opportunity, choosing family over career.

Not all competing commitments are clearly aligned with our highest values; often, these hidden forces subtly undermine our progress. Harvard Graduate School of Education faculty members Robert Kegan and Lisa Lahey have spent decades researching this phenomenon, which they term "Immunity to Change." Their method, grounded in over 30 years of adult developmental research, helps individuals uncover ingrained mental patterns that distort perceptions and block new ideas, ultimately obstructing meaningful change.

Described as a "mental X-ray," this process reveals the inner barriers that commonly hinder personal and professional growth. As Lahey explains, "Mindset transformation requires overcoming blind spots, unearthing our competing commitments, and freeing ourselves from limiting assumptions"—an essential step in addressing the deeper adaptive challenges that go beyond behavioral adjustments.[2]

Constructive Developmental Theory (CDT) suggests that as adults, our thought processes evolve, helping us see and reshape the ways we construct our own reality. Reaching higher stages of cognitive development

---

[2] Bauld, Andrew. "Changing for the Better: Immunity to Change." *Harvard Graduate School of Education*, https://www.gse.harvard.edu/hgse-100/changing-for-the-better

requires me to become aware of the beliefs and assumptions that once guided my thinking from the subconscious. I've found that part of this growth involves examining any unconscious commitments that might oppose my goals or conflict with core values I learned early in life. Carol Dweck's "growth mindset" theory supports this, showing how the beliefs we hold about ourselves can shape our potential.[3]

For instance, I remember a teacher once telling me, "You'll never be good at math." At the time, I accepted it as true, internalizing it as a fixed mindset that led me to avoid math whenever I could. But years later in university, I surprised myself by excelling in a challenging statistics course. I realized that the teacher's assessment wasn't an objective truth. It was a belief I'd adopted in that moment and it shaped my decisions for years. As Henry Ford famously put it, "If you believe you can or believe you cannot, you're right." Reassessing those limiting beliefs has helped me let go of old assumptions and opened up new possibilities for growth.

Competing commitments often surface whenever we transition to a new level or take on a more challenging role. These opportunities can bring out hidden doubts about our abilities, leading us to think, *"I'm not sure I'm good enough for this."* When this kind of self-doubt arises, we may unknowingly sabotage our own progress by finding reasons to turn down the opportunity.

---

[3] Dweck, Carol S. *Mindset: The New Psychology of Success.* Random House, 2006.

These competing commitments are frequently tied to our self-image or how we view ourselves in a particular role. For instance, imagine you're known as an expert in a specialized area within your company, where you excel and feel confident. Then, one day, a top executive invites you to step into a management role, leveraging your expertise to lead a larger team, a skill outside your comfort zone. Because you see yourself as an expert, not a manager, this self-perception becomes a competing commitment that holds you back from embracing the new role. Here, the commitment might sound like, *"I feel competent and respected as an expert, but I'm not as confident in a leadership position."* This inner conflict can ultimately lead you to turn down or unintentionally undermine the new opportunity.

The question, then, is how to move beyond these competing commitments and become an authentic leader, to become someone who is grounded in their core values and purpose. This isn't about imitating someone else's style or relying on specific traits; it's about being true to who you are. As Ann Fudge, former Chairman and CEO of Young & Rubicam, expressed, "All of us have the spark of leadership in us, whether it is in business, in government, or as a nonprofit volunteer. The challenge is to understand ourselves well enough to discover where we can use our leadership gifts to serve others." Truly authentic leadership begins with self-awareness, allowing us to understand and harness our unique abilities to make a meaningful impact.

This chapter explores two core elements in the journey to authentic leadership: purpose and values. Together, these shape your identity, your core sense of who you are. Let's begin with purpose.

The Power of Purpose

An actuary who reported to me came into my office one day with some eye-opening statistics. "Take a look at this," he said. "People who work until retirement, without any purpose or plans beyond that, often pass away within five to seven years after they stop working." I found this fascinating and kept it in mind all day. That evening, I shared it with my wife. "I have good news and bad news," I told her, showing her the data. "The bad news is, I'm never retiring. I plan to keep doing this work as long as I can."

She looked at me, a bit startled. "And the good news?" she asked.

"The good news is...I'm never retiring. I'm going to keep doing this work as long as I can."

I realized that the work I'm sharing with others is my purpose. One question I'd encourage you to ask yourself is: Do you feel a genuine connection with what you're doing day to day? Does your work give you a sense of purpose that truly resonates with you? And just as importantly, are you taking care of yourself along the way?

Years ago, my wife and I traveled to Zambia, a place we visited frequently. On one of our trips, we stopped by a local school near a village. We spoke with the headmaster and a village elder about ways we might support the school. Always insightful, my wife asked, "What's your biggest challenge?" I hadn't even thought to ask that question.

The headmaster explained, "Our biggest challenge is retaining teachers. They come here, start families, but eventually leave because we don't have a preschool. They go elsewhere to find a place where their children can learn." She immediately responded, "Why don't we build a preschool for you?" And that's exactly what we did. We helped build the preschool, and when I visited Zambia last year, I saw it still thriving. Some teachers have now been with the school for over ten years.

This experience reminded me of the power of having a purpose, especially one that goes beyond our daily routines. Finding something that speaks to you on a deeper level, that makes a lasting impact, can be a powerful way to understand and connect with your purpose.

The Power of Alignment

People often tell me, "I'm struggling to find my purpose. I don't see any clear signs, no neon lights pointing the way. I don't feel completely aligned, and life is hard." And yes, life can be challenging. I invite you to consider this: how close are you to your purpose in your daily life? You might not reach 100% alignment, but the goal is to move in that direction. If you can get to 80-90% alignment, you'll feel it. You'll feel more alive.

I'm fortunate to own my own business, which gives me the freedom to shape our values and how we operate. This makes it easier for me to align with my purpose. If you work in a corporate setting, however, ask yourself: Am I aligned enough with my purpose to feel alive in what I'm doing each day? Or am I moving away from it by being here? This simple question can bring a lot of clarity, and only you can answer it truthfully.

The questions "Who am I? Who are others? What am I to do?" have guided human wisdom for centuries, encouraging self-reflection and a search for purpose. Cultivating a clear purpose is energizing and motivating, helping us focus on what truly matters. Authentic leaders are deeply passionate about their purpose. It's not only about what they do, it's about how and why they approach their work. Purpose aligns your strengths and passions with your role, making your work both meaningful and impactful. To be effective, purpose should be specific, personal, and resonate with you alone.

Identifying Your Purpose

There are three key steps to discovering your sense of purpose:

1. Explore your life story for major themes that reveal your core passions and values.

2. Craft a clear purpose statement that truly energizes you.

Take actionable steps to bring that purpose to life.

Authentic leaders don't view themselves as victims of circumstance; instead, they reflect on past experiences to uncover what gives their lives meaning. We've all faced challenges, and these moments shape who we are. When 75 members of Stanford Graduate School of Business's Advisory Council were asked what capability leaders most need to develop, nearly all agreed: self-awareness.

Start by taking time to review your own life story. Look for common threads and pivotal experiences that have influenced your journey. Recall significant events and relationships that have shaped your perspective, and note the impact of these moments. As you do, pay close attention to recurring messages and themes, and consider the following questions:

- What was the most difficult challenge you've had to face in your life?

  ____

  ____

  ____

- What did you learn about yourself during this experience?

  ____

- When was another moment when you faced immense conflict or pressure?

- What did you learn from this experience?

- What are you most proud of in how you responded to this experience?

- Who is the most significant person in your life, and why?

- When was the last time you felt inspired? Who is someone that inspires you?

Now, take the time to look at your answers to the above and notice any patterns or themes that are emerging. Here is a list of questions to guide your thinking:

- When you look at your life experiences, what do you notice?
- What stands out?
- What patterns are there?
- What surprises you?
- What do you regret?
- What are you most proud of in general?
- What are the biggest lessons you have learned?
- Name three strengths you are particularly proud of.
- Anything else you want to add?

Now, identify the most common themes that keep surfacing in your answers and use them as a foundation to craft your purpose statement. A purpose statement captures the essence of who you are and what drives you, serving as a guiding light in your journey as an authentic leader.

For inspiration, here are some examples of purpose statements:

- To help others live more meaningful lives.

- To be the quiet, behind-the-scenes motivator who drives success.
- To be the persistent force that keeps people moving forward!

Take some time to reflect on these ideas, and write down a purpose statement that feels true to who you are:

My purpose is:

____

____

____

____

Once you've written your purpose statement, place it somewhere you'll see it often and remember it. The next step is to identify your core values. This process takes time, so be patient with yourself. Often, life's most challenging experiences reveal our highest values, illuminating what truly matters to us.

Discovering Your Core Values

I've been highly autonomous ever since I was a child. When I was six, my mom was concerned with the state of the educational system in Zambia so she decided to send me to live with my dad in Johannesburg. I boarded a train with my 14-year-old cousin, who was supposed to look after me for the journey. As it turned out,

I didn't see him again until we stepped off the train in Johannesburg!

The trip itself was an adventure, a 2.5-day journey in a sleeper carriage with four bunks. We'd run up and down the train, and the older kids would even dare to walk on the outside of the train, swinging from one car to the next. When the bell rang for meals, we'd head up to the dining car. The conductor made sure I ate, keeping a watchful eye on me, likely at my mother's request. At each stop, all the kids would jump off to explore, and the conductor would make sure I got back on.

After that, my parents grew comfortable with me traveling alone. They'd put me on the Express Motorways bus, speak with the driver, and seat me in the front, right next to him. I often made the journey from Zambia to Zimbabwe on my own, and each trip deepened my sense of independence and my belief that I could look after myself.

These experiences taught me, from a very young age, that I could take care of myself. More importantly, they showed me how much I value autonomy and freedom. These values remain core to who I am today.

Uncovering Your Core Values

The idea here is that a core part of who you are has remained unchanged since childhood, though these values often become obscured as we grow into adulthood. Reconnecting with and uncovering these values is like Michaelangelo chiseling away to reveal the unique beauty of a sculpture hidden within the stone. These distinctive qualities make you who you are, and they're worth celebrating.

Our core values are shaped by our upbringing, our experiences within the education system, and our cultural backgrounds. Most of these values are formed between the ages of 4 and 10, influenced by the environment we were raised in, our family's beliefs, and our cultural surroundings. These foundational values stay with us for life, even as we mature and change in other ways. That's why the life story exercise is so impactful: it helps us identify the people and experiences that had the greatest influence on us and understand who we were modeling ourselves after. In many ways, our past tells us a great deal about the kind of person we're meant to be in the future.

Many of us aren't fully aware of our core values. We may have never taken the time to identify or contemplate them, so they often run in the background, unconsciously shaping our reactions. Because of this, we may find ourselves reacting to situations without understanding the underlying reasons. Often, when we feel a strong reaction to something, it's because one of our values has been crossed or disregarded. It's as if someone has overstepped a boundary we're not even consciously aware of, prompting us to react instinctively.

The truth is, we can't manage what we're unaware of, which is why understanding our core values is so valuable. When Michelangelo was asked what he saw as he stood in front of a block of stone, he famously replied, "I see an angel longing to be liberated." He envisioned the angel within the rock and simply carved away the excess to reveal it. This process of uncovering our authentic selves is much the same. By chipping away at our own assumptions and unconscious patterns, we reveal the core values that truly define us. What are those unshakable values? What patterns are we running without even realizing it? Discovering these is the journey toward authenticity.

Understanding our core values gives us insight into what drives, motivates, and energizes us. For example, I tend to rebel when my core values of freedom or autonomy are restricted. I become irritable and frustrated. But because I'm aware that these values are essential to me, especially when working in a team, I can regulate my emotions more effectively and avoid reacting impulsively.

If we're unaware of our values, we can't pinpoint what's triggering our reactions, making it difficult to regulate our responses. When we understand our core values, we can act with intention, constructively advocating for what matters to us. Often, when someone crosses our boundaries, our negative reactions aren't due to their intent to harm but rather to an unintentional overstepping of a deeply held value. Recognizing our values empowers us to communicate these boundaries openly, fostering healthier interactions and more authentic connections.

To begin defining your core values, start by taking an inventory using the list of words below. Reflect on each word carefully, and circle 10-12 that resonate most with you and reflect what truly matters in your life. Next, identify the 2-3 values that you absolutely cannot live without. Put a star beside them, highlight them, and commit to remembering and honoring them. These values represent who you truly are at your core.

Values Inventory

Accountability
Accuracy
Achievement
Adventurousness
Altruism
Ambition
Assertiveness
Balance
Being the best
Belonging
Boldness
Calmness
Carefulness
Challenge
Cheerfulness
Clear-mindedness
Commitment
Community
Compassion
Competitiveness
Consistency
Contentment
Contribution
Control
Cooperation
Correctness
Courtesy
Creativity
Curiosity
Decisiveness
Democraticness
Dependability
Determination
Devoutness
Diligence
Discipline
Discretion
Diversity
Dynamism
Economy
Effectiveness
Efficiency
Elegance
Empathy
Enjoyment
Enthusiasm
Equality
Excellence

Excitement
Expertise
Exploration
Expressiveness
Fairness
Faith
Family-orientedness
Fidelity
Fitness
Fluency
Focus
Freedom
Fun
Generosity
Goodness
Grace
Growth
Happiness
Hard Work
Health
Helping Society
Holiness
Honesty
Honor
Humility
Independence
Ingenuity
Inner Harmony
Inquisitiveness
Insightfulness
Intelligence
Intellectual Status
Intuition
Irreverence
Joy
Justice
Leadership
Legacy
Love
Loyalty
Making a difference
Mastery
Merit
Obedience
Openness
Order
Originality
Patriotism
Perfection
Piety
Positivity
Practicality
Preparedness
Professionalism
Prudence
Quality-orientation
Reliability
Resourcefulness
Restraint
Results-oriented
Rigor
Security
Self-actualization
Self-control
Selflessness
Self-reliance
Sensitivity
Serenity
Service
Shrewdness
Simplicity
Soundness
Speed
Spontaneity
Stability
Strategic
Strength
Structure
Success
Support
Teamwork
Temperance
Thankfulness
Thoroughness
Thoughtfulness
Timeliness
Tolerance
Traditionalism
Trustworthiness
Truth-seeking
Understanding
Uniqueness
Unity
Usefulness
Vision
Vitality

Recognizing Value Misalignment

Now that you have a clearer sense of your core values, ask yourself: Do these values align with the work you're doing today? When values are out of alignment, it often leads to feelings of frustration, especially around decision-making and how choices are handled within the organization. You may feel that your communication isn't valued, or get a sense that "I don't fit here" or "I don't feel like I belong."

Let me share an example to illustrate how value misalignment can impact a sense of purpose at work. A client of mine was working at a healthcare company where decisions were primarily driven by profits, while her role centered on patient well-being. This created a real conflict with her values. While she understood that profitability is essential for any company, the CEO's focus on revenue over patient care made her feel as though her commitment to patients was compromised. This misalignment led to ongoing tension and frustration for her. Over time, she found herself frequently disagreeing with executive-level decisions, which only deepened her sense of not belonging.

You may be in a similar situation, staying in a job that doesn't align with your values because you're uncertain if another opportunity will come along. Financial obligations, such as a mortgage or supporting your children, often keep you in place, leading you to tolerate an environment that conflicts with your core beliefs.

Deep down, though, you know you're not bringing your best to the role. You're working out of necessity, not because you feel fully engaged or inspired by what you do.

Before moving forward, take a moment to reflect on some essential questions and answer them honestly:

- Do my organization's values align with my personal core values?
- Is there enough alignment between my values and the company's to allow me to put forth my best effort?

If the answer is no, then something has to change. As you become more aware of your purpose and core values, you'll begin to feel a new sense of ease, as if you're flowing like water down a mountain. You'll start connecting more deeply with ideas that resonate with your highest self, opening up a world of new possibilities. This awareness allows you to realize that you are not limited by the negative thoughts or "thought viruses" In your mind. You are so much more.

As Thich Nhat Hanh wisely observed, "When you take the first step, the path appears." I've seen this truth unfold time and again with clients. When they take that first, sometimes challenging step toward their purpose, the path begins to reveal itself, with opportunities and insights emerging along the way. They find that as they align with their true values, even small actions lead them forward, proving that transformation begins with commitment.

A Holistic Approach to Leadership

As you move forward, remember that obstacles are inevitable. Building a strong foundation doesn't mean you'll reach your goals overnight; patience and persistence are essential. Effective leadership starts with embracing your authentic self. But true impact requires more. You must lead as a whole person, engaging your head, heart, and gut. In the next chapter, we'll explore how to connect with these three centers of wisdom, empowering you to lead with deeper insight and purpose. This journey begins by honoring all parts of who you are.

KEY INSIGHTS

- Authenticity is the foundation of true leadership. Aligning your actions with core values builds resilience and clarity, particularly during moments of conflict or high pressure.
- Knowing your purpose fuels impactful decisions. A clear sense of purpose energizes leaders to create meaningful connections and inspire others.
- Value alignment enhances fulfillment. When your work reflects your values, you lead with greater motivation, empowering others to create a ripple of positive change.

CHAPTER 4:

WHOLE-PERSON LEADERSHIP: BALANCING THE HEAD, HEART, AND GUT

An individual's ideal state is achieved when they fulfill the purpose for which they were born. And what does reason demand of them? Something very simple—that they live in harmony with their own nature.
–Adapted from Seneca the Younger

Authentic leadership is about leading as a whole person. This chapter explores how integrating your head, heart, and gut enables more balanced decision-making and fosters deeper connections with your team.

In the early stages of your career, you're often focused on mastering your own skills, performance, and individual contributions. Picture yourself as a violinist in an orchestra: you practice tirelessly, refine your craft, and ensure your part is flawless. As you grow, you might be promoted to lead violinist, taking on the responsibility of coordinating with others in your section. While still focused on your performance, you begin to experience the first notes of collaboration.

Leadership demands a broader transformation. As you rise to more senior roles, the focus shifts from "me" to "we." This represents a transformation in perception rather than a need for new skills. You realize it's not just about learning new techniques; it's about changing how you see the world and your role within it.

Your perspective widens to encompass not just individual parts but the entire orchestra. Now, you're the conductor. It's no longer about playing a single instrument perfectly; it's about creating harmony among diverse players. You guide the musicians through complexity, competing commitments, and never-ending change, ensuring that every note contributes to a cohesive whole. In this role, chaos is your challenge, and mastery lies in your ability to bring order and meaning, amplifying your impact across the orchestra.

This evolution from individual contributor to conductor is not about acquiring entirely new skills. It's about transforming how you see yourself and your role within the larger ensemble. Authentic leadership calls for you to engage the whole person: your logical head, empathetic heart, and intuitive gut to lead with clarity and resonance in an ever-disruptive world. Let's explore how you can orchestrate your leadership for maximum impact.

The Evolution from "Me" to "We" and Beyond

In leadership, transitioning from a "me" to a "we" mindset (and ultimately to an "it" mindset, where the focus is on the organization) represents a profound shift in perspective. Moving beyond personal impact, leaders begin to consider what benefits the team, and eventually, the organization as a whole. This transition can dramatically reshape careers and team dynamics, fostering a broader, more inclusive approach to decision-making.

For example, a new manager may initially focus on how their success is measured by individual achievements. Yet as they grow, they start to ask, "What's the impact on us as a team?" and "How does this benefit the organization?" This broader viewpoint shifts from personal advancement to actions that empower and support the collective, aligning with organizational goals. Leaders who embody this mindset are often seen as transformative, prioritizing the organization's long-term success over short-term personal gains.

The Challenge of Operating from Whole-Person Wisdom

Making this shift is challenging because we tend to rely predominantly on our heads, our logical center. Ninety percent of decision-making often comes from an analytical perspective, overlooking the other centers of wisdom: the heart and the gut. This can lead to one-sided decisions that lack emotional intelligence and instinctual insight. By engaging the heart and gut along with the head, leaders can draw from a complete state of being, accessing richer, more balanced information.

For instance, when data alone drives decisions, it can inadvertently emphasize short-term metrics at the cost of long-term sustainability. Boosting quarterly results might look good on paper, but it could erode team morale or undermine the organization's core mission. Focusing solely on metrics also risks fostering a culture of compliance over innovation, reducing employees' contributions to mere numbers rather than meaningful insights and impactful solutions.

Balancing Data with Emotional and Instinctual Wisdom

Over-reliance on data-driven decision-making can also fail to capture crucial elements like market shifts and customer sentiment, potentially leading to out-of-touch strategies. Leaders must balance analytical input with an awareness of the organization's mission and values. Otherwise, they risk incentivizing behavior that conflicts with these principles. For instance, if metrics dominate, some may take shortcuts, focusing on immediate wins that compromise integrity and long-term impact.

While some leaders operate from a data-driven, analytical perspective, others may lean entirely on purpose or intuition, both of which present challenges. Purpose-driven leaders may overlook the necessary structure and processes required for strategic initiatives, while those who rely primarily on gut instincts may neglect team insights, leading to inconsistent decisions that confuse stakeholders and reduce team buy-in.

Exercising Whole-Person Decision-Making

Effective leaders cultivate the ability to use their head, heart, and gut in harmony. Analytical data provides essential insights, but it must be balanced with empathy and intuition to create well-rounded strategies. This whole-person approach enables leaders to respond thoughtfully to challenges, adapt to shifts, and communicate decisions in ways that inspire trust and foster a shared vision.

An exercise to support this could involve scenario analysis: envisioning a common workplace issue and considering how it affects "me," "we," and "it." By walking through this model, leaders can practice making decisions that both achieve results and nurture a healthy team culture and organizational growth.

As leaders embrace the "we" and "it" perspectives, they gain a broader understanding of their role in shaping the organization's culture and long-term vision. This journey is not about acquiring new skills alone; it's about shifting how we perceive our impact. Leaders who approach their roles from a whole-person perspective make choices that resonate with team members, align with organizational values, and drive meaningful, sustainable change.

Exercise: Aligning Head, Heart, and Gut for Balanced Decision-Making

Use this exercise to approach a decision with a whole-person mindset, drawing insights from your head, heart, and gut for a balanced, thoughtful choice.

1. Choose a decision you need to make soon where you'd like to be intentional about using all three centers of wisdom.
2. Head: Begin with facts and data. Write down key information related to your decision. Ask yourself, "What does the information tell me?"
3. Heart: Place your hand on your chest, tune into how the decision feels emotionally, and ask, "How does this align with my values or the team's purpose? Who will benefit or be affected by this?"
4. Gut: Take a deep breath, place your hand on your stomach, and listen to your instinctive response. Ask, "What gut sense do I get about this decision? Does anything feel especially right or wrong?"
5. Review your responses for each center. Observe how each perspective contributes to your understanding. Notice any misalignment. There will be an important insight in that response. Pay attention to that. Does one perspective stand out more

than others? How does balancing all three inform your next steps?

By following this process, you'll bring greater alignment and clarity to your decision-making, helping you create choices that are balanced, informed, and values-driven.

Take Off the Mask

My hope is that you see the same version of me show up every time. Whether you're reading this book, watching me speak, or joining me in a live training session, I aim to be the same person each time, every week, month in and month out. I'm not here to put on a performance or pretend to be something I'm not; I'm here to show up authentically, without the need for pretense.

Of course, there have been times when I wasn't fully myself. After losing my late wife, Deb, I was weighed down by grief and stress, and in those moments, I wasn't as soft or present as I wanted to be. It happens to all of us; there are times when we put the mask back on, times when we feel safer hiding our true selves. And that's perfectly natural. Vulnerability can be daunting, and sometimes we need that mask as a temporary shield. Eventually, however, if we want to grow and evolve, we have to take it off.

For me, showing up as my true self means grounding in the belief that "I'm OK" just as I am. It means accepting my feelings, recognizing that the intrusive thoughts I experience aren't truly mine, and embracing my whole self without judgment. When you start to embrace that part of yourself, you'll notice that the same authentic person shows up every time. You begin to show up consistently for others because you're being real. No masks, no pretense. And often, when you lead with this authenticity, your gut instincts will find support in the facts, and your purpose will feel aligned with what you're doing.

Engaging All Centers of Wisdom

Working from the whole person means using all our centers of wisdom, the head, the heart, and the gut, to make better, more informed decisions. Start by asking, "What does the data tell me? What do the figures show?" This is the foundation. Yet you can go deeper by asking, "What is my heart telling me about this?" Simply placing your hand on your heart and tuning in can reveal insights or new information that logic alone might miss. When both the head and heart are aligned, move to your gut. Place your hand there and ask, "What do I instinctively feel about this? Is there something I should be cautious about?" Often, this reflection leads to an inner signal or alert that adds depth to your decision-making process.

Paying attention to these subtle signs is like filtering information through three distinct channels, each offering valuable perspective. When you align your head, heart, and gut, you operate as a whole person, which tends to result in clearer and more balanced choices.

Rather than relying solely on logic or data, consider: What does my heart say about the right course of action? What does my gut sense? By taking all three perspectives into account, you create a foundation of integrity in your decisions.

There's also a cautionary element here. Data can sometimes be misleading or incomplete due to collection methods, biases, or assumptions. Over-relying on it without consulting our other centers can lead to decisions we later regret. Balancing all three centers prevents this, offering a more holistic view. Many times, I've seen clients solely focused on metrics and numbers ask, "What does the data show?" When I respond with, "What is your gut telling you?" they're often surprised and taken aback. They may have never thought about including their gut feelings in a professional decision. When they do, it usually leads to insights they hadn't considered.

For example, a client might say, "My gut says there's something I need to think more about," prompting them to pause and reflect further. By listening to all parts of themselves, they often uncover valuable information, leading them to say, "Wow, I never thought about it that way before."

Our heads, hearts, and guts are all channels through which we receive information, yet most organizations encourage leaders to rely heavily on their heads alone. This can create a narrow perspective, missing the valuable, nuanced information our other centers of wisdom provide. Embracing all three enables a higher level of functioning and leads to better, more balanced decisions.

Case Study: Patagonia's Holistic Decision-Making

Patagonia exemplifies the whole-person approach by integrating data, emotional intelligence, and intuition into their decision-making processes. Their "Don't Buy This Jacket" campaign, launched on Black Friday in 2011, challenged traditional corporate growth strategies and showcased their commitment to environmental sustainability.[4]

This move was backed by robust data and sustainability metrics, showing that Patagonia's products, made with durable and sustainable materials, outlasted competitors' offerings. Their leadership relied on both quantitative analysis and an intuitive understanding of their brand identity and emotional connection with their customers. This gut instinct, informed by their mission to "cause no unnecessary harm," aligned with their belief that this provocative message would resonate with their audience's growing environmental awareness.

By trusting their employees' alignment with the company's mission and encouraging an open dialogue about

---

[4] Uri Neren, "Patagonia's Provocative Black Friday Campaign," *Harvard Business Review*, November 23, 2012, https://hbr.org/2012/11/patagonias-provocative-black-f.

the campaign's potential risks and rewards, Patagonia's leadership demonstrated emotional intelligence. The campaign ultimately succeeded in deepening customer loyalty and advancing Patagonia's mission, proving that decisions driven by the head, heart, and gut can achieve remarkable results.

This illustrates that when organizations take a holistic approach, they create outcomes that are both profitable and deeply aligned with their values. Patagonia's blend of data-driven strategy, emotional resonance, and intuitive clarity sets a benchmark for how leaders can integrate multiple wisdom centers in their decision-making.

Operating from the Whole Person

Operating from the whole person means using the Head, Heart, and Gut as three distinct centers of wisdom in decision-making. Each center brings a unique perspective: the Head focuses on logic and data, the Heart aligns decisions with purpose and values, and the Gut relies on intuition and past experience. Leaders who integrate all three can make well-rounded decisions and connect more authentically with those around them. The chart below offers insight into each center, along with questions to help leaders reflect on where they naturally lead from and how they can achieve balance across all three.

Operating from the Head	**Operating from the Heart**	**Operating from the Gut**	**Balancing Head, Heart, and Gut**
Leaders who primarily use their Head prioritize data, facts, and logical analysis. This approach can result in overthinking or an over-reliance on ego. To balance, consider incorporating more Heart-based questions. **Questions to Consider:** *- What does the data tell us?* *- What are the facts?* *- What do I get out of this?*	Heart-centered leaders focus on values, purpose, and the well-being of others, often finding unique solutions and strengthening relationships. Practicing Heart-based leadership can broaden insights and connect on a deeper level with others. **Questions to Consider:** *- How does this align with our purpose?* *- What feels right in this situation?* *- Who benefits from this decision?*	Leaders who rely on the Gut use intuition and experience to make choices. While powerful, Gut-only leadership may miss data or overlook team input. Balancing the Gut with Head and Heart perspectives ensures well-rounded decisions. **Questions to Consider:** *- What do my instincts tell me?* *- What does my experience suggest?* *- Does this feel like the right choice?*	Using all three centers together enables leaders to make comprehensive, balanced decisions and connect authentically with others. Reflecting on where you naturally operate from can help you integrate all three perspectives in your leadership approach. *Aim to tune into all three centers to connect fully with others and make balanced, values-aligned decisions.*

Balancing Head, Heart, and Gut in Leadership Conversations

Imagine a CEO who meets weekly with his VP of Operations. The CEO notices that, despite talking a big game, the VP consistently fails to deliver on promises. Although the CEO is aware of the VP's poor performance, he hasn't yet addressed it.

If the CEO were to approach this situation purely from the head, he might go straight to the facts. He'd likely say, "Your performance is unacceptable," and follow up with data showing the VP's failure to meet targets. This straightforward, data-driven approach leaves little room for understanding or support and might alienate the VP, making it harder to motivate them toward improvement.

Now, if the CEO were to approach from the heart, he'd reach out and try to understand what might be causing these performance issues. He might say, "We value your contributions, but I've noticed things aren't going as planned. What's happening on your end?" This approach invites open dialogue, allowing the VP to share any personal or professional challenges that may be affecting their work.

Lastly, if the CEO relied only on his gut, he might sense something is off but lack concrete evidence or clear direction on how to address it. Acting on a vague feeling of dissatisfaction, he might express frustration without a clear plan or specific feedback. This approach risks coming across as reactive or abrasive, which could hinder productive dialogue and make the VP defensive.

Instead, using all three centers can help the CEO communicate more effectively. He could start by acknowledging the data (head), express concern and openness (heart), and check in with his instincts about the VP's potential for improvement (gut). This balanced approach is more likely to lead to constructive outcomes, fostering both accountability and collaboration.

Following My Inner Guidance: How a Simple Yes Led to a Major Win

A few years ago, I was invited to speak at a mentoring program in Zurich. The program director said, "We can't pay you, but would you be willing to speak?" My initial reaction from my head was, "I should be paid for this. I'm a professional speaker." Fortunately my gut sensed potential, thinking, "This could be an opportunity," while my heart felt aligned with the program's purpose and wanted to support the director's work. So, I replied, "Yes, I'll speak. I don't need a fee, but could you cover my flight and accommodation?" She agreed, and I added one more request: "Could you also arrange a meeting with Kim, your CEO, in the afternoon?" She said yes, and we set it up.

The next day, I flew to Zurich, launched the program, and it went exceptionally well. Around lunchtime, Kim, the CEO, arrived, greeted me warmly, and expressed her excitement about our upcoming meeting, hinting that she had a question for me. Later, when we met, she shared, "I'd love for you to lead a coaching masterclass for our international team and deliver it in multiple languages." Smiling, I agreed, saying, "We can definitely make that happen."

Afterward, Kim asked, "So, what did you want to discuss with me?" I replied, "Actually, I was hoping to propose running the Coaching Masterclass internationally." She laughed and said, "That's perfect!"

What resulted was one of the largest contracts our company has ever had, involving global travel and delivery in 11 different languages. This success came from listening to all my centers of wisdom. My intuition recognized an opportunity, my heart valued the program's mission, and my head ensured we met on practical terms. When we align our whole person in decision-making, we're more receptive to messages that can lead us to incredible opportunities.

Embracing Authentic Identity

To lead from your whole self, you must first understand who you truly are and allow that identity to shine through consistently. This means showing up as the same person in every setting, whether in your personal life or at work.

Start with these questions: Who am I? How do I show up? What are the words that best describe me? If I asked five close friends to describe me, what words would they choose?

For example, you might say: I am a generous, courageous, authentic leader who strives to make a positive impact. Embracing an identity like this enables others to see your core values in action.

The world is eager for authentic leaders, those willing to take off the masks and show up as their true selves. As Brené Brown famously notes, "In order for connection to happen, we have to allow ourselves to be really seen. You have to be willing to let go of who you think you should be." When you allow your authentic self to emerge, you inspire others to do the same, fostering genuine connection and unlocking your full potential as a leader.

As we deepen our practice of whole-person leadership, using our head, heart, and gut in harmony, the impact of our choices extends beyond personal insight to influence the entire team and organization. Yet bringing this authentic approach to life is not without challenges. Most organizations have unwritten rules and cultural expectations that subtly shape behaviors. In the next chapter, we'll explore these 'unspoken rules' and discover strategies for aligning values with actions in a way that nurtures an authentic, thriving culture.

KEY INSIGHTS

- Whole-person leadership promotes balance. Integrating logical, emotional, and intuitive wisdom enables leaders to make thoughtful, well-rounded decisions.
- Inclusive leadership strengthens teams. Shifting from a "me" to a "we" mindset fosters collaboration and enhances organizational success.
- Core values build trust. Embodying and communicating your values consistently creates transparency and connection with your team.

CHAPTER 5:

THE UNSPOKEN RULES: ALIGNING CULTURE WITH VALUES

The value of culture is its effect on character. It avails nothing unless it ennobles and strengthens that. Its use is for life. Its aim is not beauty but goodness.
—W. Somerset Maugham

There are visible rules in every organization. Yet it's often the unspoken expectations that truly define its culture. These unspoken rules can create friction for leaders striving to show up authentically, subtly shaping behaviors in powerful ways. In this chapter, we'll explore how these hidden dynamics operate and how aligning them with our core values can foster a more authentic, values-driven environment.

Many organizations hold cultural expectations that discourage leaders from showing up as their true selves, creating a disconnect between personal values and organizational demands. One client illustrated this well during the COVID crisis. When asked what he had learned while working remotely, he shared, "I've come to know my people far more intimately than when we worked in the office. Now, I balance tasks and relationships, focusing on building stronger connections." This shift happened through remote meetings, where he began to see colleagues as whole people who introduced him to their families, pets, and personal lives. This new level of connection allowed him to lead from a place of genuine support.

If we're willing to embrace it, sometimes a change in environment can open the door for authentic connection. Still, many organizations continue to prioritize results over relationships, even if leadership rhetoric says otherwise. Leaders often feel caught between their desire for authentic connection and a corporate culture that demands results at any cost. The message from the CEO might be, "Our people come first," but the pressure from top leaders tells a different story.

I've spoken with hundreds of leaders working remotely, and they often share a similar wish: "We don't want to lose the closeness and intimacy that virtual work has brought." Yet, many organizations quickly revert to a culture of "deliver at all costs," overshadowing the importance of people and relationships. In such cultures, the idea that "the task comes first" can override authentic leadership, which damages both the team and the company. This thought virus that performance always trumps people spreads quickly and quietly, shaping the organization's culture unless challenged.

Aligning Rewards with Desired Behaviors

A critical issue in shaping company culture is the misalignment between what is said and what is rewarded. Leaders often talk about the importance of collaboration, innovation, and respect, but if the rewards structure only recognizes individual performance, people will naturally prioritize that over teamwork and creativity. A board or CEO may emphasize collaboration, but if compensation is tied solely to production, the behavior will lean toward personal gain over group success.

One CEO I coached acknowledged this disconnect. When asked about his biggest challenge, he said, "We need more innovation to adapt to constant change." I then asked, "What happens if someone tries something new and makes a mistake?" He replied, "We punish them." This response revealed why innovation was stagnant in his company. By punishing mistakes, the culture stifles experimentation. Instead, companies should view mistakes as learning opportunities, asking, "What did you learn, and what will you do differently next time?" This approach fosters a culture of innovation and creativity.

Embracing Failure as Part of Innovation

For true creativity to thrive, leaders need to embrace a culture that encourages controlled experimentation.

Failure is integral to innovation; as ideas evolve, they improve. Companies that wait for a perfect product miss out on learning that comes from early iterations. A culture that encourages releasing early and "building the plane as we fly it" inspires risk-taking and innovation. Leaders play a crucial role in setting this tone.

As leaders, our job is to shape a culture that balances task and relationship. If we see that task completion is prioritized at the expense of human connection, we need to speak up and say, "We're damaging our business by putting tasks before relationships." This involves being true to yourself and having the courage to address behaviors that are harming relationships and stifling innovation. When leaders embody this authenticity, they empower others to follow suit, creating a culture that values both the task and the human experience.

The Emotional Contagion Effect

Emotional contagion is a powerful process through which emotions spread from one person to another, creating a shared mood and impacting group dynamics and behaviors. In their influential book *Emotional Contagion*, authors Elaine Hatfield, John Cacioppo, and Richard Rapson describe this phenomenon, noting that "people tend to align with the emotional state of the other person, in terms not only of emotionally empathizing with the other but also of mimicking facial expressions and coping with bodily changes."[5] This alignment happens subconsciously, as we pick up on others' cues and adjust our own emotions accordingly, reinforcing a collective emotional experience.

Recent studies suggest that emotional contagion is not confined to in-person interactions. In an experiment involving Facebook users, researchers manipulated the emotional content displayed in users' News Feeds to observe its impact on their posting behaviors. When positive content and emojis were minimized, users posted fewer positive updates and instead expressed more negative emotions. Conversely, when negative content was reduced, users' posts became more positive. This study underscores that even in digital spaces, where physical cues like facial expressions and tone of voice are absent, emotional contagion persists. Emotions transmitted through online networks can influence the moods and behaviors of others within the network.

The findings suggest that emotional contagion operates across both physical and digital domains, shaping individual emotions and the collective atmosphere in online communities. This effect highlights the importance of emotional awareness and positivity, as even brief interactions can have a lasting impact on the emotional landscape of a group.

[5] Hatfield, E., Cacioppo, J. T., & Rapson, R. L. (1994). *Emotional Contagion*. Cambridge University Press.

The Power of Emotional Contagion

When leaders are comfortable being themselves, they grant others permission to do the same. The emotional contagion effect operates like an unspoken message: "If I'm okay, you're okay." By modeling self-acceptance, leaders foster a culture where team members feel safe to express their authentic selves, which in turn promotes trust, collaboration, and genuine engagement. When everyone feels accepted, differences are valued, and the team can focus more effectively on their collective goals.

Emotional contagion can also work negatively. In high-pressure environments where the unspoken message is to "deliver at all costs," people are often placed second, fostering an atmosphere of fear and anxiety. Even if leaders don't explicitly say, "Make us money, customers come first," this sentiment can become the default attitude, infecting the organization and impacting behavior in unproductive ways. In such environments, the pressure to perform and the fear of underperformance spread quickly, creating a ripple effect of stress and disengagement.

This process is driven by mirror neurons, which respond to the emotions and actions we observe in others. When a leader experiences and exhibits fear, for example, their team unconsciously picks up on and reflects that same anxiety. In this way, the leader's emotional state sets a tone that can either inspire and uplift or, if negative, create a culture of tension. Leaders who consciously manage their emotions, especially in high-stress environments, can foster a positive and resilient team culture, leveraging the emotional contagion effect to cultivate confidence and well-being across the organization.

How to Use the Emotional Contagion Effect in Positive Ways

Many people tend to focus on identifying what went wrong, but celebrating achievements, no matter how small, can have an even more profound impact. Go out of your way to acknowledge the successes of others and provide meaningful recognition. For some, regular acknowledgment is essential. When you receive positive client feedback, take the time to highlight it and express gratitude to the person responsible with a simple, "Thank you so much."

I consistently make it a point to thank my team. For example, I'll say, "Thank you for the great work you've done; what we delivered for this client was superb, and the team effort was truly impressive." By regularly validating and appreciating others' contributions, you create a positive emotional contagion effect, uplifting morale and inspiring continued excellence.

Build Trust Through Vulnerability and Open Dialogue

Beyond recognition, fostering trust and connection is equally important. One strategy is to facilitate vulnerability-based trust through personal storytelling. Encouraging team members to share pieces of their life story, for example, such as family dynamics or formative experiences, can help humanize each other and build stronger emotional bonds. For instance, during a team-building exercise, you might ask, "Where did you grow up? What role did your siblings play in your life?" Such exercises expose shared humanity, even in the face of disagreements.

When disagreements arise, focus on how the team operates rather than solely on the content of the disagreement. Establish clear norms and principles for respectful interaction: *How do we challenge each other constructively? How do we disagree respectfully?* Teams that agree on the "how" often find it easier to navigate the "what."

Create Space for Genuine Connection

As a leader, I've also found value in hosting open-ended, agenda-free check-ins. When asked, "What's the agenda for today?" I might reply, "There's no set agenda. I just want to check in, see how everyone's doing, what's going well, where we might improve, and how things feel on a day-to-day basis." These unstructured moments often create space for genuine sharing. For instance, a team member might say, "I'm struggling; my daughter is going through a tough time." I respond by asking, "What do you need? How can we support you? What can we do to help ensure you and your family are okay?" These conversations foster authentic connection and demonstrate care that extends beyond the workplace.

Facilitate Constructive Dialogue in Group Discussions

When moderating group discussions, especially in moments of overlap or conflict, it's critical to model active listening and provide a framework for constructive dialogue. For example, if several people are speaking at once, I might pause the conversation to say, "Let's hear from one person at a time so everyone feels heard. [Name], can you start, and then we'll go around?" This ensures inclusivity and encourages thoughtful contributions, creating an environment where people feel valued and respected. It creates a ripple effect of positivity, reinforcing a culture where people want to collaborate, share ideas, and support one another.

Caring for the Whole Person

I believe in a psychological contract with my team: if you're in trouble, I'm here to help. A few months ago, someone I highly value in my business faced a crisis where her sister was recovering from a serious car accident. They were struggling to find the right physical therapy support, hitting barriers at every turn.

So, I asked her, "What do you need?" She hesitated and said, "I know I haven't met my work commitments recently, but if possible, I need some financial help to get the care we need." Within three minutes, the funds were in her account. I told her, "Send me the bills. What matters is that your sister gets the right support."

We provided financial support beyond the usual to ensure her sister received proper care. Today, her gratitude and loyalty are beyond words. This isn't about buying loyalty. It's about showing up authentically. Generosity, compassion, and authenticity are core to who I am, and I'd want someone to do the same for me in a time of need. Going the extra mile for her wasn't calculated. It was a reflection of my values, and I believe she'll remain loyal to our team not because of the money, but because we were there for her when it mattered most.

Regulation and Self-Control

The first step to preventing the spread of negative emotional contagion is self-regulation. As authentic leaders, it's essential to take responsibility for how we react and respond to circumstances, both in our professional and personal lives. The small yet crucial gap between reacting and responding can dramatically impact the dynamics of any environment.

Imagine your spouse says something that triggers you, and you feel the urge to argue. Reacting immediately often escalates the situation, as it allows the "inner child" to take control, expressing frustration without fully understanding what's being said. At that moment, you're not really hearing them. You're reacting, which can lead to misunderstandings and conflict.

Instead, when you feel that surge of emotion, take a step back and allow yourself a pause. A deep breath, a few seconds of calm, can give you the space to respond thoughtfully rather than react impulsively. This short pause shifts you from reacting emotionally to responding mindfully, creating a powerful way to regulate emotions. This approach is essential for engaging others intentionally and constructively. Many relationship issues arise from immediate reactions rather than measured responses, so practicing self-regulation helps foster more positive and productive interactions.

The acronym STOP is a powerful tool for maintaining self-control in high-stress situations. STOP stands for:

- **S**tep back
- **T**ake a breath
- **O**rganize your thoughts
- **P**roceed mindfully

There are times when stakes feel high, and in those moments, frustration or anxiety can quickly lead to reactive behavior. Without realizing it, I might project my stress onto others, amplifying the tension for everyone involved. When I feel frustration building, I remind myself to take a breath and put things in perspective: "This is not life or death."

Using STOP helps me create that crucial pause to step back, take a breath, and organize my thoughts, so I can respond with a calm, measured approach. When I feel frustration building, I lower my voice, which grounds me and opens the door for a more constructive, solution-focused response.

This pause also enhances my listening. I'll often say, "If I'm hearing you correctly, this is what you're saying..." By clarifying the message, I gain a new perspective, allowing me to respond rather than react. Many times, strong emotions surface when we feel our values are being overlooked or disrespected. If I sense I'm being taken advantage of, it's natural for my "inner child" to feel threatened and want to push back. The inner child reacts out of self-preservation, seeking immediate relief or recognition. At the same time, the more mature part of me reminds me, "Patience. There's no need to react impulsively. I can respond thoughtfully and effectively instead." This balanced approach creates space for growth and mutual understanding in any interaction.

Nonviolent Communication

Sometimes, people may unintentionally trample on your identity or values without realizing it. For instance, imagine a colleague casually dismissing an idea that resonates deeply with your core values, not knowing the significance it holds for you. In such moments, it's natural to focus on the impact this has on you and to have a strong reaction, as your sense of self feels threatened. This is when speaking up to honor what matters most to you can be empowering, as it helps uphold the most authentic version of yourself.

In cases like this, applying Nonviolent Communication (NVC) techniques can be especially helpful. Developed by Marshall Rosenberg, NVC encourages expressing how specific words or actions affect you without assigning blame, which fosters understanding rather than defensiveness. For example, you might say, "When you dismissed my idea, I felt undervalued, as if my perspective didn't matter. What I would prefer is to discuss this in a way that respects both of our views." According to Rosenberg, "When we express our needs, rather than attacking others, we open the door for more empathetic communication."[6]

By framing the conversation in terms of your feelings and preferences rather than accusations, you give the other person the chance to clarify or reconsider their

---

[6] Rosenberg, Marshall B. *Nonviolent Communication: A Language of Life*. PuddleDancer Press, 2015.

actions. Often, they may respond with surprise, saying, "I didn't mean it that way," which allows you to express how their words impacted you and opens the door for a respectful dialogue about boundaries and mutual respect.

In contrast, there are times when a reaction arises automatically without really touching on your values or identity. Here, the reaction may be a reflex rather than a defense of something core to who you are. When this happens, pause and ask yourself: "Am I reacting just to be right, or am I aiming for a constructive outcome?" This moment of self-awareness allows you to consider what truly matters and to respond in a way that aligns with your larger goals, rather than engaging in unnecessary conflict.

Changing the Rules

To navigate unspoken rules effectively, leaders must be willing to change them. One common mistake, especially among CEOs of large corporations, is assuming that a culture can be shaped by simply stating values like "integrity" and "fairness" without aligning rewards and incentives to reflect these ideals. This creates a disconnect between the stated culture and the actual behaviors within the organization.

For instance, imagine a banking environment where "integrity and fairness" are displayed prominently on the walls as core values. While these values might look inspiring, they don't match the reality of how employees are incentivized. If compensation and rewards are tied solely to the amount of money employees bring in, then "integrity" becomes secondary, even irrelevant, to the daily operations and decisions of the team. When incentives prioritize profit over values, employees are more likely to adopt behaviors that maximize earnings, regardless of integrity. To truly change culture, organizations need to align what they reward with the values they wish to uphold.

A CEO might declare that integrity and honesty are essential values and must guide the company's operations. However this vision won't materialize without adjusting how employees are incentivized. Take the 2008 banking crisis as an example: despite the existential threat to the financial system due to reckless behavior, within a year, traders were back to receiving the same high-risk, profit-driven bonuses. What impact do you think that had on the culture?

If Wall Street traders' compensation structures remain unchanged and everyone on the trading floor accepts that this is simply how things work, then that reward system effectively defines the culture. No matter what a company says about its values, there will always be friction if rewards are misaligned with the behaviors and principles the organization wants to promote. When incentives clash with declared values, employees will prioritize what they're rewarded for, and the culture will reflect that, not the company's stated ideals.

Often, chief executives approaching retirement focus heavily on maximizing sales and boosting share prices, knowing they'll cash out their shares when they leave. This kind of short-term incentive doesn't necessarily drive sustainable growth. Once they've cashed in, they're done. This mindset is starting to shift. More companies are tying executive bonuses not only to what leaders achieve but also to *how* they achieve it. They are increasingly asking, *Did you achieve results ethically?* This focus on values-based performance reinforces a culture that prioritizes both results and integrity.

A notable example is Alex Gorsky, the retiring CEO of Johnson & Johnson, who emphasized the importance of aligning incentives with company values. As he stated, "Our Credo is a living and breathing document. It's both timely and timeless."[7] This approach helps keep leaders like Gorsky invested in the long-term success of the organization, encouraging them to build sustainable value even after their tenure. By structuring compensation to reflect both outcomes and the manner in which those outcomes are achieved, Gorsky's model demonstrates how restructured incentives can drive ethical behavior, ensuring the alignment of leadership actions with organizational values.

---

[7] Johnson & Johnson, https://www.jnj.com/latest-news/johnson-johnson-ceo-alex-gorsky-reflects-on-the-power-of-the-companys-credo.

Activity: Designing Values-Driven Incentives

Use this activity to assess and align your team's incentives with the values you want to promote within your organization:

1. List the top three values that define your team or organization (e.g., integrity, collaboration, innovation). These values should represent the behaviors and principles you believe are crucial for long-term success.
2. Look at your current reward and incentive structures. Do these structures encourage behaviors that align with your values, or do they inadvertently prioritize other goals, such as short-term gains over teamwork? Identify any gaps or misalignments.
3. Choose one core value, such as collaboration, and recognize an incentive that reinforces this behavior. For example, if your goal is to strengthen collaboration, consider implementing team-based rewards or publicly celebrating cross-departmental projects.
4. Introduce your values-driven incentive on a trial basis. Take note of any shifts in behavior, morale, or engagement, and observe how well this incentive aligns your team with your organization's mission and values.

This exercise will help you create a work environment that consistently rewards values-driven behavior, ensuring that your team's actions reflect the principles you most want to see in your culture.

In this chapter, we've explored the hidden dynamics of organizational culture and how misaligned incentives, unspoken rules, and the emotional contagion effect can shape the behavior of leaders and teams. When leaders align their behaviors, rewards, and communication with their core values, they create an environment where collaboration and teamwork flourish. Next, we'll examine the key factors that drive high-functioning teams. The journey toward a culture of authenticity continues, and it begins with understanding the crucial role trust plays in shaping performance and relationships.

KEY INSIGHTS

- Culture reflects priorities. Aligning incentives with desired values ensures that employees' behaviors reinforce what the organization truly prioritizes.
- Leadership communication drives morale. Emotional contagion and authentic communication from leaders create either a culture of positivity or one of stress.
- Balanced incentives support growth. Leaders who value relationships and innovation over short-term results promote sustainable success and stronger team dynamics.

CHAPTER 6:

BUILDING TRUST: THE SECRET TO HIGH-FUNCTIONING TEAMS

The quality of your culture is determined by the quality of your relationships, and the relationships depend on the quality of the conversations.
–Judith E. Glaser

One of the greatest challenges leaders face today is the assumption that everyone is on the same page. Often, it's not just about what tasks we're tackling or the problems we're solving, but *how* we're working together. The foundation of a high-functioning team lies in asking the essential question: "How do I bring out the best in my people?"

A good starting point is to engage directly with your team members and ask, "What support do you need from me to do your best work?" To uncover genuine insights, it helps to adjust your perspective. Step into your employees' shoes and ask yourself these questions:

- Is my leader trustworthy?
- Do I trust my leader to act on what we need to succeed?
- Is trust something that must be earned, or is it given?

You'll likely discover that trust means different things to different people. For some, trust must be earned through consistent actions; for others, it may be given freely until broken. Understanding where each person stands allows you to tailor your approach, setting clear expectations for how to nurture and build trust with each team member.

The Role of Trust in Team Performance

Here's what's critical to understand: trust is the linchpin of efficiency and success. Stephen Covey, a leadership expert and author of *The Speed of Trust*, emphasizes that trust is a measurable and actionable asset with a direct impact on both speed and cost.[8] When trust is low, productivity slows, and operational costs rise. Conversely, when trust is high, the speed of production increases dramatically, and costs decrease significantly. Simply put, the trust you cultivate with your people is one of the most significant drivers of both profitability

---

8 Stephen M.R. Covey, *The Speed of Trust: The One Thing That Changes Everything* (New York: Free Press, 2006).

and operational ease. Once you establish trust, your business becomes more profitable, and your operations flow more smoothly. It's important to note that building trust is not a one-time effort. Trust is an ongoing commitment that pays dividends over time.

The following framework outlines key steps for defining expectations, demonstrating trustworthiness, and fostering open dialogue. These steps provide a roadmap for cultivating trust within teams and ensuring long-term success.

Trust-Building Step	**Specific Actions**	**Impact**
Define Expectations	- Clarify what trust means for you and your team. Is it earned? Is it given? - Discuss mutual expectations around behavior, communication, and accountability.	Establishes a shared understanding of trust, reducing ambiguity and preventing assumptions.
Demonstrate Trustworthiness	- Align your actions with the agreed expectations. - Be consistent, reliable, and transparent in your behavior.	Builds credibility and reinforces the team's confidence in your leadership and commitment.

Foster Open Dialogue	- Create opportunities for ongoing conversations. - Actively listen, ask thoughtful questions, and provide space for honest feedback.	Encourages transparency, strengthens relationships, and helps address issues before they escalate.

THE SPEED OF TRUST

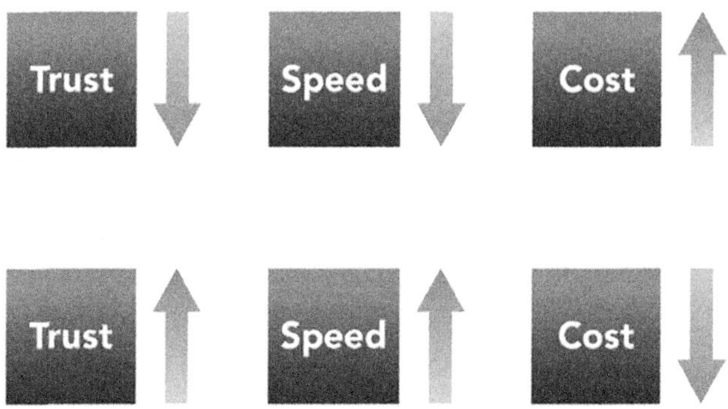

[Graphic from Stephen Covey - probably makes sense to re-create a new infographic here for your book]

Creating Safety for Dialogue and Innovation

Fostering trust within your team starts with creating an environment where individuals feel physically, emotionally, and psychologically safe. Amy Edmondson, a leading expert on organizational behavior, defines psychological safety as "a shared belief held by members of a team that the team is safe for interpersonal risk-taking."[9] When safety is absent, people tend to default to reactive behaviors driven by survival instincts. This reactive state stifles creativity, collaboration, and problem-solving, which are essential for any team to thrive. The best ideas often come through some amount of friction. To unlock the full potential of your team, it's crucial to establish a culture where taking risks, sharing ideas, and contributing authentically are not only accepted but encouraged.

A cornerstone of this process is engaging in what we call "uncommon dialogue." This means going beyond superficial conversations and fostering communication that addresses deeper needs, concerns, and aspirations. Judith Glaser, an organizational anthropologist and author of *Conversational Intelligence*, explains how transformative conversations strengthen connections, build trust, and pave the way for collaboration and innovation.[10] She argues that uncommon dialogue requires leaders to listen actively, ask thoughtful questions, and create space for vulnerability. When people feel genuinely seen, heard, and valued, they move from

---

[9] Amy C. Edmondson, *The Fearless Organization: Creating Psychological Safety in the Workplace for Learning, Innovation, and Growth* (Hoboken, NJ: Wiley, 2019).
[10] Judith E. Glaser, *Conversational Intelligence: How Great Leaders Build Trust and Get Extraordinary Results* (New York: Bibliomotion, 2014).

a reactive state to a responsive one. This lays the foundation for innovation, trust, and long-term success.

A Rare Dialogue

In my experience working with over 20,000 leaders globally, I've consistently posed the same question: "How many of you have discussed with your team what trust means to you and to them?" Astonishingly, in more than two decades, just 23 leaders affirmed having such a conversation. Only twenty three. Less than 0.2% of people that I have surveyed said they've had a conversation with their people about what trust means to them and their people.

Given that trust is fundamental to high-functioning teams and relationships, this lack of dialogue is perplexing. Trust is not a one-size-fits-all concept; it varies among individuals. For instance, I operate on the belief that team members will proactively communicate issues early, allowing for timely solutions. Yet others may view trust differently, perhaps as something to be earned over time.

To bridge these differences, it's essential to engage in open conversations about trust. Ask team members, "How can I earn your trust? What actions would demonstrate trustworthiness to you?" This dialogue clarifies expectations and fosters mutual understanding.

Additionally, it's vital to discuss communication preferences. Inquire about preferred methods and frequencies of communication. Does your team prefer email, phone calls, or messaging apps like WhatsApp? Understanding these preferences ensures that important information is shared effectively, further strengthening trust within the team. By initiating these uncommon dialogues, leaders can cultivate a culture of transparency and collaboration, laying the groundwork for stronger, more cohesive teams.

Psychological Contracts and Safety

Once we agree on the rules of engagement, it's important to maintain those rules and that agreement. Unfortunately, this doesn't always happen. The idea of a psychological contract is to establish a shared agreement about how we want to work together. These agreements clarify mutual expectations, which is essential for building trust and fostering engagement within teams. When these expectations are clear, trust flourishes, and team members feel secure enough to contribute fully. But when assumptions replace clear agreements, trust breaks down, leading to disengagement and frustration.

The Danger of Assumptions

This is what happens 99.9% of the time: as a leader, I assume Joe will do certain things in a certain way. I've created a picture in my mind of how Joe will show up. And when Joe doesn't meet those expectations, I get irritated. Rather than addressing it directly, I avoid the conversation entirely. Over time, I withdraw from Joe because he's not operating as I hoped. Joe, in turn, notices my change in demeanor and begins to wonder, "What's going on with the boss?"

At this point, the situation escalates. I read an email from Joe one day, and something he wrote triggers me. I get angry, explode, and scream at Joe. Later, I calm down, apologize, and reset. Everyone assumes we're fine, but we're not. The cycle repeats, unresolved, over and over again. Nothing gets fixed.

This kind of dynamic leads people to leave companies. When employees don't feel safe in your presence or don't trust you, they say things like, "My boss isn't paying attention to me," or, "They don't value my contributions." Eventually, they leave, and you lose talented people because of unspoken expectations and damaging assumptions.

Building and Maintaining Trust

If someone veers off from the original agreement and starts behaving in ways that weren't agreed upon, trust begins to erode. People no longer feel safe. Your behavior must align with the agreement, and as long as it does, things run smoothly. When you notice that someone is acting contrary to what you agreed upon, it's time for another conversation. Address the issue, reset expectations, and create a new psychological contract. This process must be ongoing. The most effective organizations have these conversations regularly, yet they are often avoided entirely.

Allow me to share an example. When I transferred to a business unit in London, the new chairman and I didn't get along. He micromanaged my every move, and as someone who values autonomy, this became a problem. I was technically competent and good at what I did, but his constant oversight frustrated me to no end. Finally, I realized we needed to have a conversation.

I approached him directly and said, "I can't work with you under these circumstances. Here's what I would prefer: I'll handle clients, the technical aspects of our business, and the team. You handle finance, investor relations, and the rest. Let me focus on delivering for the clients and the team, and I'd prefer you leave those aspects to me."

It wasn't an easy conversation, but we agreed. We didn't become friends, but we respected each other's strengths and boundaries. This psychological contract allowed me to get the autonomy I needed to do my work effectively. It's a concrete example of how these conversations can improve trust and productivity.

The Cost of Avoiding Conversations

Avoiding these pivotal conversations often leads to reactive behavior. If you're the leader of a team and fail to explain how someone can earn your trust, they won't know what you expect. Misalignments will grow, especially with difficult or destructive individuals. The solution? Have those conversations, reset expectations, agree on mutual goals, and clarify how you want to operate together.

In effective relationships, these discussions happen regularly. Communication is a two-way street. By striking a psychological contract, you ensure both sides get what they need. Once the agreement is made, it's your responsibility to honor it as best you can.

When trust is high, things happen quickly and efficiently, often at a lower cost. When trust is low, everything slows down. People second-guess themselves, seek excessive approvals, and hesitate to take action. This lack of trust creates a drag on productivity and drives up costs.

Creating Psychological Safety

Every person has an inner child, and if that inner child doesn't feel safe, they'll retreat. People become reactive, hesitant, and unproductive. If it's unsafe to make mistakes, people won't experiment or innovate. However, in a high-trust environment, engagement and discretionary effort increase. When people trust you and you trust them, they grow, develop, and deliver their best work. Mistakes become learning opportunities rather than sources of fear.

Trust isn't automatic. You must have conversations about what trust means. Ask: What does trust mean to you? What does it mean to me? Do I give trust freely, or must it be earned? Different perspectives and expectations exist, and if we're reactive to those differences instead of responsive, relationships will falter. For less trusting individuals, it's important to understand their criteria for giving trust. The faster you can build trust, the sooner you'll collaborate effectively and succeed together.

Listening to Understand

My hope is that people who meet me see the same person show up in any circumstance. I am collaborative, I am curious, and I am happy to state my point of view while also listening to others. Listening to understand does not mean I necessarily agree, but it gives us a solid foundation for discussion and ensures we can achieve great things together.

Remember, you want to be the conductor. It's your job to accept that everyone will see things differently, and that's okay. While it can slow things down and even be frustrating at times, slowing down to consider everyone's perspective often leads to better thinking and stronger solutions.

The Cost of Dismissing Perspectives

As a big-picture thinker, I'm not risk-averse. When I have an idea, I often think, "Let's go!" Still, I rely on people around me to push back and say, "Wait a second. We don't have enough data or clarity yet." For example, if someone on my team says, "You haven't taken this into account," and I respond with, "I don't care," that person won't feel seen or heard. They'll feel disrespected.

Such a dismissive response breaks down trust and psychological safety. When team members don't feel their perspectives matter, their performance suffers. They begin to ask themselves, "Is this a place where I can grow and develop?" If the answer is "No," they'll start looking for opportunities elsewhere.

Instead, if I respond by saying, "Tell me more about that. Help me understand your perspective," I give them the space to feel seen and heard. This is vital because being seen, heard, and valued is one of the most important needs for human beings. When team members feel that their voice matters, they stay engaged and committed.

Listening Without Agreeing

Listening to understand doesn't mean agreeing. Once I've heard a team member's perspective, I might still say, "I've heard you and understand your concerns, but I think this is the best path forward." The key is demonstrating that I've listened carefully, understood their point of view, and taken it into account before making a decision. This approach builds trust and influence, as it shows respect for their input.

On the other hand, when leaders interrupt, dismiss, or defend their own perspective without hearing others out, it erodes trust. Comments like, "I know best," or, "I'm in charge," signal that their perspective is the only one that matters. Such assumptions create a toxic environment where people stop sharing their thoughts, and the quality of decision-making declines.

The Power of Mutual Respect

Great leaders build the habit of listening to all perspectives before making decisions. While the final decision may rest with the leader, the process of engaging with different viewpoints ensures better outcomes. If people see you consistently listening, taking their input into account, and making thoughtful decisions, they will respect your leadership.

This is particularly important because, in many cases, the people you lead are closer to the action than you are. Their insights can provide critical information to help you make the best decisions. Dismissing these perspectives alienates your team and ultimately limits the quality of your decisions.

A Lesson in Engagement

I remember a client I was working with a few years back. I was coaching his team, and we had come together for a meeting where different parts of the team were presenting their ideas on a particular theme the client had asked them to work on. We started the meeting, and the leader was just sitting there. He wasn't reacting to any of the ideas in the presentations. He wasn't asking questions and came across as somewhat dismissive.

His team started to get agitated. One of his team members pulled me aside and said, "Wow. Are these ideas terrible? What are we doing wrong? I thought he would love these concepts, but he doesn't seem to be interested." The whole team felt like they hadn't done a good job. After the first presentation, we took a tea break. I took the leader aside and said, "What's going on with you? These guys are worried and upset that you're not responding to their ideas. You haven't asked any questions, and you seem uninterested. Is everything okay?"

The leader looked at me and said, "Frans, I'm sorry. I went out late last night and had a bit too much to drink. I'm really struggling today. I think the presentations are fantastic."

I replied, "Oh good, because you're not engaging with them the way you normally would. Please understand the impact you're having by operating like this."

The leader took some headache tablets, had a big coffee, and came back. This time, he was in much better shape. After the next set of presentations, he addressed the team and said, "I'm really sorry. I wasn't feeling very well this morning, but I'm feeling better now. I'm sorry I didn't respond positively earlier, because I think your presentations are fantastic. You've had some great ideas."

The moral of the story: never assume. Listening to understand can build mutual respect, increase psychological safety, and let the people you're working with know that their views matter. It shows that you hear them and value what they have to say.

Nelson Mandela's Approach to Listening

A fantastic example of listening to understand comes from Nelson Mandela. When asked what he learned about leadership from his father, Mandela shared how his father would always be the last to speak during tribal meetings. His father wanted to hear everyone's perspectives first, gathering all the facts and ideas before offering his own view. By listening intently, Mandela's father ensured that decisions were fair and informed.

This principle of being the last to speak allows leaders to demonstrate they've understood and appreciated everyone's perspective. It ensures decisions are based on the collective wisdom of the group.

The Distinction That Builds Trust

When I listen intently and show I've understood someone's perspective, it doesn't mean I agree with them. But it opens the possibility that they'll listen to me in return. If I dismiss their perspective outright, they're unlikely to consider mine. Listening to understand creates a foundation of mutual respect and collaboration, which is critical for effective leadership.

Great leaders demonstrate that they've truly heard and valued the people they work with. Whether or not they agree, the act of listening fosters psychological safety and trust, enabling teams to perform at their best.

Psychological Contracts: Having Conversations That Foster Trust

Building trust within any team or organization requires intentional and structured communication. A key strategy is forming psychological contracts, or informal agreements based on mutual understanding and respect. These contracts are about clarity, accountability, and the shared belief that everyone's contributions matter. If we want others to trust us, we must ask what we can do to earn that trust and then follow through with actions that reinforce our commitment.

When preparing for pivotal conversations, a structured approach can make all the difference. The SCARF model (Status, Certainty, Autonomy, Relatedness, and Fairness) provides a framework for fostering trust and creating psychological safety. By addressing these five core human needs, you can tailor your communication to reduce fear and build stronger connections. Here's how each driver plays a role:

- Status: Reinforce the value of each person's contributions.
- Certainty: Set clear expectations to reduce anxiety.

- Autonomy: Encourage input and decision-making.
- Relatedness: Build rapport and shared purpose.
- Fairness: Ensure equity in treatment and feedback.

By incorporating these principles, you can navigate conversations with greater trust, mutual respect, and psychological safety. Here's how both initiators and recipients can approach these conversations effectively:

Tips for Initiators:

1. Start with Positive Intent: Show respect and a genuine desire to improve the relationship or situation. This sets a collaborative tone.
2. Use Specific Behaviors and Examples: Focus on observed actions, supported by data if possible, rather than generalizations.
3. Describe Effects on Others: Help the recipient understand the broader implications of their actions.
4. Clarify and Validate Understanding: Ensure your feedback is understood by summarizing and confirming key points.
5. Set Clear Expectations: Be specific about the changes you hope to see, without assuming you're entirely correct.
6. Listen Actively: Validate the recipient's feelings, and observe their emotional and behavioral responses.
7. Commit to Support: Share how you'll help support the new behavior moving forward.

8. Ask for Clarification: Be open to feedback on your own role in the situation and reflect on how you may have contributed to the outcome.
9. Summarize and Confirm: Close the conversation by recapping agreements and ensuring mutual understanding.

Tips for Recipients:

- Reflect on how your contributions are valued (Status).
- Seek clarity on what happens next (Certainty).
- Ask for autonomy and involvement in decision-making (Autonomy).
- Emphasize collaboration and shared goals (Relatedness).
- Ensure perceived fairness in the process (Fairness).

Moving Forward

Leading pivotal conversations is not just about addressing issues. It's about building lasting trust. By preparing thoroughly, framing discussions with respect and purpose, and leveraging tools like the SCARF model, you can transform challenging moments into opportunities for growth and connection.

Trust is not built in a vacuum. It flourishes when leaders expand their focus beyond individual interactions and begin orchestrating the collective strengths of their teams. As you deepen your capacity for authentic leadership, the next step is to shift your perspective from being a high-performing individual to becoming the one who empowers others to thrive.

This is the focus of the next chapter: transitioning from a soloist to a conductor. It's about evolving your leadership identity from personal achievement to collective impact, mastering the art of collaboration, and guiding your team toward shared excellence.

KEY INSIGHTS

- Trust fuels organizational success. High trust enhances efficiency, reduces costs, and fosters a foundation for innovation and collaboration.
- Psychological safety enables creativity. Leaders must create environments where team members feel safe to speak, take risks, and learn from mistakes.
- Dialogue strengthens relationships. Regular, open conversations about expectations and communication preferences build stronger team cohesion.

CHAPTER 7:

FROM SOLOIST TO CONDUCTOR: THE EVOLVING LEADER'S JOURNEY

The conductor of an orchestra doesn't make a sound. He depends, for his power, on his ability to make other people powerful. –Benjamin Zander

When transitioning from an expert achiever to a catalytic leader, you undergo a profound change in identity. The focus shifts from being about *you* to being about *others*. This transformation is about expanding your range of capabilities in new and exciting ways. It's about moving from being an expert to becoming an orchestrator, to becoming someone who gets people to collaborate seamlessly.

The journey from an individual contributor to a catalytic leader can be likened to the evolution of a musician in an orchestra. At the start, you are like the violinist, focused solely on mastering your own craft. Your role is clear: deliver excellence through your personal expertise, dedication, and skill. Success at this stage is measured by the quality of your individual performance, your ability to solve problems independently, and your consistent output. The mindset of the violinist is centered on individual performance and self-improvement, with behaviors that are task-oriented and self-reliant.

As you grow, you transition to the role of the lead violinist. Here, you take on a hybrid position that combines personal performance with a new layer of responsibility: guiding and mentoring others. While you still contribute directly, your focus expands to helping your team align their individual contributions toward a shared goal. Much like ensuring the string section plays cohesively, you work to harmonize the efforts of those around you. This stage requires a delicate balance between your personal contributions and your responsibility to coordinate and support the team. You begin to provide feedback, foster collaboration, and even delegate tasks, though it may be tempting to retain some control over the process.

Eventually, the journey leads to the role of the conductor, where your focus shifts entirely to the big picture. You are no longer playing an instrument yourself; instead, you are orchestrating the entire team to achieve harmony and excellence. Amid the chaos that often defines modern leadership environments, the conductor brings order and direction, transforming potential discord into a cohesive and purposeful performance. Your primary responsibility is to create a compelling vision, set clear expectations, and empower others to perform at their best.

The mindset of the conductor is deeply rooted in trust and the belief that empowering others brings out their greatest potential. Your behaviors reflect this trust: you actively create an environment where people feel valued, align their efforts with organizational goals, and innovate without fear of failure. At this stage, your success is no longer defined by your personal output but by the collective achievements of your team. This progression illustrates the profound transformation that occurs as you move from focusing on individual expertise to enabling and empowering others to excel.

Why Leadership Requires a New Mindset

Most of us enter the workplace as individual contributors, excelling in a specific area of expertise. When you're highly skilled at something, your supervisor or even the organization's President might say, "Congratulations! We want you to manage a team with this expertise. Here's your promotion." When people are promoted, however, they often fall into the trap of thinking they need to control everything. This mindset stems from their prior success, which was largely based on *their* actions and *their* ability to deliver results. They've been recognized for solving problems directly, so naturally, they assume their new role will demand more of the same.

Managing a team isn't "more of the same." If you bring that same mindset of individual achievement to your new role, you risk alienating your team. Your workers may feel you don't have their backs, aren't giving them the space to do their best work, and aren't trusting them to succeed. This controlling approach often leads to disengagement and diminished effort.

As your team begins to feel micromanaged, their internal dialogue shifts: *"You don't trust me. You don't see me. You're not listening to me. You only care about the tasks, not about me."* That breakdown in trust comes at a high cost. Your need to control everything stifles your team's potential and pushes people away.

This happens because we make assumptions about how others work, often based on our own experiences, work history, and upbringing. The belief of, *"I know best. I have experience. I got this promotion because I'm in charge,"* is one perspective. If left unchecked, however, it can erode relationships, destroy team morale, and ultimately undermine your business. True leadership requires letting go of the need to control and embracing the art of enabling others to succeed.

Transitioning from a controlling leader to an empowering one requires a deep level of self-awareness. Daniel Goleman, a psychologist and author best known for popularizing the concept of emotional intelligence, explains that "self-awareness is the foundation of emotional intelligence."[11] Understanding one's own triggers and tendencies allows leaders to manage their reactions and connect authentically with their teams.

People Love Being Treated As Adults

Over the past 45 years, both as an insurance executive in senior leadership positions and in my years of experience in executive education, I've observed one of the most challenging transitions for managers: expanding from managing to leading. When we are asked to lead a team, it often seems like we develop amnesia and forget what we valued most from the leaders who treated us well and fostered our growth. These leaders treated us as adults.

Not everyone is ready to become a catalytic leader. One major reason is that the transformation of identity involved can feel unsafe. Early in my career, as a 25-year-old, I was fortunate to have an incredible manager. He treated me as an adult, fostered my creativity, and helped me grow by having regular conversations. He pointed out where I could improve and asked how I could be even more effective. That experience empowered me when I earned my first management position. I told my team I would treat them as adults. I wouldn't clock-watch, and in turn, I expected the same

[11] Daniel Goleman, *Emotional Intelligence: Why It Can Matter More Than IQ* (New York: Bantam Books, 1995).

from them. My only request was that they ensure our clients were taken care of and that their work was up to date. Beyond that, they could manage their time as they saw fit.

Trust Creates Discretionary Effort

I told my team, *I won't clock-watch you. I'll treat you as adults. You come to work, do your job, and whether you work remotely or in the office, I trust you to manage your responsibilities.* If someone came in late, I trusted there was a good reason, perhaps a sick child or a personal errand. My only criteria were that our clients were satisfied, their needs were met, and our service remained exemplary.

This trust formed the basis of a strong psychological contract. While other divisions in the company operated strictly on a 9-to-5 schedule, my team worked with greater flexibility. They often came in early or stayed late because they felt empowered and trusted. That discretionary effort wasn't something I demanded; it was something they chose to give. For example, one team member once informed me she'd be late due to a doctor's appointment. I told her, "You don't need to tell me. I trust you. As long as your work is up to date and our clients are happy, you're free to manage your time."

Letting Go to Foster Innovation

If you look at the big picture of moving from violinist to conductor, there is a risk leaders must take. You have to trust that your people will deliver what's required without you dictating every step. While you might know how you would execute a task, leading means embracing the possibility that someone else may approach it differently. This difference is not just acceptable. It's valuable. It brings new perspectives and ideas to the table.

This shift requires treating people as adults while ensuring strong psychological contracts are in place. These agreements establish the expectations for how your team will operate together, serving as a guiding force for a collaborative and co-creative relationship.

When we trust others to bring their unique strengths and take ownership, we empower them to find their own solutions and share their gifts. This doesn't mean lowering standards. In fact, It's about holding people to high standards while allowing them the freedom to innovate and deliver results in their own way. For many leaders, this leap of faith is difficult because it requires relinquishing control over how tasks are executed. Yet, clinging to control can create bottlenecks that stifle creativity and innovation.

When leaders let go, set clear outcomes, and provide a compelling vision, they enable their teams to operate in their most creative and effective states. This is the essence of becoming a catalytic leader: helping others excel without micromanaging them.

Adopting a Coaching Mindset

Leading change is one of the most valuable skills you can develop. The only way to do this effectively is by taking others with you. Think of yourself as a custodian of culture. You shape the culture of your organization by how you lead. One of the most impactful ways to nurture talent is to adopt a coaching mindset. Instead of relying on the traditional "command and control" approach, move toward asking questions and fostering inquiry. This is where innovation and creativity truly thrive.

To put this mindset into practice, there's a key concept you must embrace: the best ideas often come from the people around you. These individuals are closer to the product, your clients, and the day-to-day realities of your business. Their insights are invaluable, and they can add tremendous value to your organization. By remaining open to their ideas and encouraging their contributions, you unlock a wellspring of innovative solutions.

This approach is a departure from traditional leadership models that dictate, "You must tell your people what to do" or "You need to shape their thinking." While leaders often take pride in being the go-to expert with specialized knowledge, this mindset can inadvertently stifle growth. Of course, your expertise is critical, and your contributions are essential. But the coaching mindset invites you to contribute differently. It allows you to create an environment where others can grow, innovate, and excel.

From Specialist to Enabler: Redefining Your Role

Leaders who act as specialists, like violinists in an orchestra, often control every aspect of their work. While this can feel rewarding in the moment, it creates a bottleneck that hinders team growth, scalability, and innovation. When everything depends on you, your organization struggles to flourish.

The fear of stepping back and not having all the answers can be daunting. You may worry about losing control or your sense of value. The truth is that adopting a coaching mindset can lead to greater fulfillment. By creating conditions where your team generates solutions, you'll experience a renewed sense of purpose and excitement. Watching your team light up with enthusiasm and achieve their best work is deeply rewarding. This is the role of the evolving leader.

The Power of Buy-In and Empowerment

It might seem more efficient to simply tell your team what to do, but this approach often backfires. When directives come solely from the leader, team members may lack full understanding, belief, or both. This can lead to repeated conversations and diminished engagement.

By contrast, the coaching mindset fosters buy-in because the ideas originate from your team. When people feel that their contributions matter and that they're growing personally and professionally, they're far more engaged. Empowering your team to do their best work satisfies fundamental human needs: the need to grow, to develop, and to feel that one's work is meaningful.

Leaders who wish to cultivate a strong sense of purpose in their teams must focus on the 'why' behind their actions. Simon Sinek, a renowned leadership expert and motivational speaker, explores this concept in his influential book *Start with Why*. Sinek argues that "people don't buy what you do; they buy why you do it."[12] By clearly articulating a compelling purpose, leaders inspire their teams to align their efforts with a shared vision.

Your technical skills got you to where you are today, and they're a source of well-earned pride. Now it's time to balance those skills with the ability to develop others. The greatest leaders are more than just experts. They're catalysts for growth. That's how you evolve as a leader and create an organization that thrives.

---

[12] Simon Sinek, *Start with Why: How Great Leaders Inspire Everyone to Take Action* (New York: Portfolio, 2009).

Reflecting on Leadership: Setting the Standard

To satisfy the need for growth and to become a leader who inspires loyalty and development in your people, start by asking yourself these questions:

- *Am I creating a culture of continuous development for my team?*
- *Do I encourage and support those who want to grow?*
- *Am I, as a leader, creating space for that growth to happen?*

Leadership development is as much about remembering as it is about building new skills. Take a moment to reflect on the leaders who influenced your own journey:

- *Who saw your potential and supported your growth?*
- *Who invested in you and backed you when it mattered most?*
- *What skills, behaviors, and attributes made them exceptional role models?*

Think about how these leaders showed up for you:

- *Did they micromanage you or give you the autonomy to make decisions?*
- *Did they appreciate your unique contributions?*
- *Were they genuinely invested in your development and success?*

Great leaders consistently exhibit attributes that leave a profound impact on those they lead. One of these is the ability to create an environment where individuals feel safe to express themselves and take risks without fear of judgment. Great leaders also excel at fostering empowerment. They offer both support and challenges that push people to grow beyond their perceived limits. Another hallmark of great leadership is validation, or the genuine appreciation and recognition of individual contributions. This makes team members feel valued and motivated. Finally, great leaders serve as a source of inspiration. They help others see their own potential and believe in their ability to achieve more than they thought possible.

The Leader's Influence on Culture

A leader's behaviors set the tone for the entire team. To cultivate a culture of excellence, it is essential to maintain high standards and clearly define what you expect and what is unacceptable. Creating systems for growth is equally important; putting structures in place that encourage development ensures that positive changes are both implemented and sustained. When you lead by example and embody the attributes of the great leaders who inspired you, you reflect those values in your interactions with your team. By setting the right standards and reinforcing them through consistent actions, you foster an environment where everyone can thrive.

Team Alignment Exercise

Bring your team together and facilitate a discussion to clarify your shared purpose, identity, and values. Use the following guiding questions to shape the conversation:

1. What's our common purpose? *Discuss the overarching goal that unites and motivates the team.*
2. How do we describe ourselves from an identity point of view? *Define the team's identity and how it sees itself within the organization or broader mission.*
3. What are our core values as a team? *Identify the principles and beliefs that guide your decisions and actions.*
4. What skills do we have? *Take inventory of the team's current strengths and capabilities.*
5. What skills do we need? *Determine areas for growth and skill development to meet future challenges.*
6. What behaviors will support our core values? *Define the actions and habits that align with and reinforce your shared values.*
7. How would you describe the environment we are trying to create? *Envision the culture and working atmosphere the team wants to foster.*

KEY INSIGHTS

- Leadership is a transformative journey. Moving from an individual contributor to a catalytic leader requires empowering others through trust and collaboration.
- Empowerment unlocks team potential. Trust-based environments encourage ownership, innovation, and discretionary effort.
- A coaching mindset inspires growth. Leaders who ask questions and foster inquiry build engagement and create a culture of excellence.

FINAL THOUGHTS:

EMBRACING AUTHENTIC LEADERSHIP FOR A THRIVING FUTURE

It is easier to act your way into a new way of thinking than think your way into a new way of acting.
–Richard Pascale

Throughout this book, we've explored the transformative power of authentic leadership, not as an unattainable ideal but as a practical and actionable framework for personal and organizational growth. In a disruptive world where constant change offers endless opportunities for growth, authentic leadership is about aligning with your purpose, embracing your unique identity, and dismantling the barriers that hold you back. It's about showing up as your whole self to create trust, foster collaboration, and drive sustainable success.

When you lead authentically, you build trust in yourself and in others. You create an environment where people feel safe to contribute their best, unburdened by the need to hide or conform. You switch from managing tasks to inspiring people. Authenticity isn't just about being consistent, it's about being courageous enough to be real, even when it's uncomfortable.

We've seen how thought viruses, those insidious beliefs that undermine confidence, can cloud your leadership. These mental roadblocks aren't truths; they're stories we've absorbed over time. Recognizing and reframing these thought patterns is the first step toward reclaiming your authentic power. By letting go of these limiting beliefs, you open the door to clarity, confidence, and a renewed sense of purpose.

Leadership is a holistic practice. It requires more than logical decisions; it demands alignment of the head, heart, and gut. These three centers of wisdom guide balanced, empathetic, and impactful actions. When these elements work together, you transcend transactional leadership and create meaningful connections that inspire and sustain.

We've also explored the exhausting toll of wearing masks. Adapting to every room or expectation drains your energy and erodes your authenticity. By committing to showing up consistently as your true self, you break free from this cycle. This is where authentic leadership shines.

Authentic leadership is more than a personal transformation. It's a cultural revolution. When you embody authenticity, you model behaviors that ripple outward, inspiring others to lead with integrity and purpose. This ripple effect creates teams that collaborate deeply, organizations that innovate boldly, and communities that thrive on trust and openness. Authentic leadership is not just a tool for success; it's a legacy that reshapes the world around us.

Why This Matters

In a world marked by rapid change, uncertainty, and increasing complexity, the need for authentic leadership has never been more urgent. Burnout, disengagement, and misaligned cultures are symptoms of leadership that prioritizes outcomes over relationships. Shifting the focus to authenticity bridges these gaps, creating spaces where individuals can thrive, teams can collaborate effectively, and organizations can achieve lasting impact.

This book has offered a practical roadmap for navigating these challenges. The lessons here are not confined to boardrooms or management roles. They apply to every sphere of influence, from the smallest team to the largest enterprise. Authentic leadership is the cornerstone of a thriving future.

Your Journey Begins Now

As you close this book, ask yourself: What does authentic leadership look like in your life? Is it initiating a vulnerable conversation, questioning a belief that no longer serves you, or committing to consistently showing up as your true self? These seemingly small actions are the building blocks of a transformative journey.

Authenticity is not a destination; it's a daily practice. Each day presents an opportunity to lead with integrity, align your actions with your values, and inspire others by being unapologetically yourself. Leadership is not defined by titles or roles but by the way you show up in the world and engage with those around you.

To deepen this practice, consider building the habit of daily reflection. At the end of each day, take a few moments to ask yourself:

1. *What did I do really well today?*
2. *What could make it even better?*
3. *What will I do differently tomorrow?*

These simple questions can help you celebrate your strengths and identify areas for growth. Pay attention to the patterns that emerge and use them as a guide for continuous improvement.

Imagine what's possible when authenticity becomes the norm. Picture workplaces where people feel empowered to bring their full selves, organizations where collaboration replaces competition, and communities grounded in trust and shared purpose. This is the future of leadership: one where success is measured not just by what we achieve but by how we show up for ourselves and for others.

The world is waiting for leaders who have the courage to be real. By committing to authenticity, you unlock your potential and inspire those around you to do the same. Together, we can create a new generation of bold, authentic leaders who make a lasting impact.

Your journey begins now. Take what you've learned, integrate it into your life, and watch as your leadership transforms your own path and the lives of those around you. The future of leadership starts with you.

Frans Campher is a highly respected executive coach, trainer, and facilitator with over 20 years of experience helping leaders thrive. He has worked with CEOs, senior executives, and leadership teams from top global organizations in both public and private sectors. His clients include industry leaders like BP, Citibank, Deloitte, Ford Europe, GlaxoSmithKline, and Johnson & Johnson.

Frans's coaching style is transformative. He helps clients identify their strengths, build self-awareness, and achieve lasting results. High achievers turn to Frans to reflect on their successes, tackle challenges, and plan for the future.

As CEO and US President of a successful coaching and leadership development organization, Frans draws on his 28-year career in international insurance and risk management. His past roles include CEO of a European company and Non-Executive Chairman of a London financial services firm, giving him a unique ability to connect with leaders on a practical level.

Frans combines insight with action. His coaching delivers clarity, stronger leadership presence, and improved team performance. Clients describe his approach as challenging yet supportive, with real-world impact like sharper priorities, higher retention, and better business results.

As co-developer of the *Leader as Coach Masterclass*, Frans has facilitated learning for over 18,000 participants globally, earning outstanding feedback. He also teaches at Imperial Business School London, where he leads programs on leadership and coaching for executives and MBA students.

Frans holds multiple certifications, including Professional Certified Coach, Certified Integral Coach®, and Leadership Agility Practitioner. He is committed to empowering leaders to navigate challenges, inspire teams, and unlock their full potential.

Printed in Dunstable, United Kingdom

72687186R00080